POINTS OF POWER

POINTS OF POWER

Discover a Spirit-Filled Life
of Joy and Purpose

Yolanda Adams

with Lavaille Lavette

FaithWords

New York   Boston   Nashville

Scripture quotations noted NIV are from the Holy Bible, New International Version®. Copyright © 1973, 1978, 1984 by International Bible Society. Used by permission of Zondervan Publishing House. All rights reserved.

FaithWords
Hachette Book Group
237 Park Avenue
New York, NY 10017

www.faithwords.com
Printed in the United States of America

First Edition: January 2010
10 9 8 7 6 5 4 3 2 1

FaithWords is a division of Hachette Book Group, Inc.
The FaithWords name and logo is a trademark of
Hachette Book Group, Inc.

Library of Congress Cataloging-in-Publication Data

Adams, Yolanda.
Points of Power : discover a spirit-filled life of joy and purpose /
Yolanda Adams, with Lavaille Lavette.—1st ed.
p. cm.
Audience: "Filled with personal anecdotes and life-altering advice,
POINTS OF POWER empowers readers to face trouble with confidence
in a God who never fails"—Provided by the publisher.
ISBN 978-0-446-54578-5
1. Christian life. 2. Christian life—Prayers and devotions. 3. Holy
Spirit. 4. Power (Christian theology) I. Lavette, Lavaille. II. Title.
BV4501.3.A333 2010
248.8—dc22
2009023552

This book is lovingly dedicated to the bravest woman I know:
Mrs. Carolyn Adams,
my mother.
She taught me how to live life to the fullest
and never take those who love you for granted.
Thanks, Mom!

Contents

Chapter Four: The Power of Confession

Chapter Five: The Power of Praise

Chapter Six: The Power of Confident Assurance

Chapter Seven: The Power of Prayer

Chapter Eight: The Power of Peace

Chapter Nine: The Power of Protection

Chapter Ten: The Power of Victory

Acknowledgments

God—thanks for all the opportunities to be Your voice in the earth.

Taylor—my sunshine and my joy. My prayer is that I make you proud of me.

My awesome family—for all your love and support, I thank you.

Attorney Ricky Anderson—for believing all I want to do is possible.

Larry Jones, Marcus Wiley, and Anthony Valary—waking up to work with you guys is a joy! You guys make these Points live!

Lonnie McBride and Steve Bracey—for the unselfish dedication and giving, on a daily basis.

Rhonda Burnough—my best friend, who challenges me to stay focused and box-free.

Lavaille—for making sure my deadlines were met! Thanks for working with my fruitful schedule!

Pastor Ed and Lady Saundra Montgomery—thanks to both of you for pouring grace and love into my life. Irreplaceable!

Pastor Dave Roberts—for encouraging me every day to be my best self.

Pastor Tim Storey—thanks for rekindling the fire of innocence within me! You are my friend!

Bishop T. D. Jakes—thanks for imparting wisdom and

encouragement in South Africa. Who knew I would need it upon landing back in the U.S.?

Pastor Bill Winston—the deposit you made and continue to make in my life has strengthened me beyond words. I owe you lots of offerings!

Dr. Creflo Dollar—"It starts with a decision." These words ring constantly in my spirit. Thanks for lifting me to a decision!

To every apostle, bishop, first lady, church mother, and prayer partner who ever spoke into my life, thank you from the bottom of my heart.

To everyone who has heard the "Points of Power" on *The Yolanda Adams Morning Show,* thanks for the e-mails and encouragement. You pushed me to the greatest level of study. I have such joy delivering these quick studies every morning to help you understand the great love God has for you. More than anything, His plan for you is so much bigger than your most outrageous dream! Take hold of it! As A.V. always says, "Live in expectation"!

Hug somebody, love somebody—who knows, it may be the only hug that person gets today. Laugh out loud, live passionately, but most importantly, live on purpose!

A Note from Yolanda

My Points of Power are meant to encourage, uplift, and provide comfort. Trying to comprehend God's power and God's grace can sometimes be a bit overwhelming. Just how powerful God is was made clear to me through meditation. I thought of ways to best harness God's power—the power the Holy Spirit gives to us. As I studied God's Word, I began to gather different points that helped me understand how I could live my life based on God's power and grace. I often reflected on words like *faith*, *love*, and *forgiveness*. As I continued to pray and meditate, words like *confession*, *praise*, *confidence*, *prayer*, *peace*, *protection*, and *victory* were revealed to me. Those words led to the formulation of my ten Points of Power.

My Points of Power have become a benchmark for my syndicated radio show, *The Yolanda Adams Morning Show*. Twice every morning, I encourage and inspire my listeners with an uplifting discussion of the Word of God. I have received so many requests for CDs and books containing the information presented in my daily radio study, "Points of Power," that I was compelled to make this information available for all to access daily. My prayer is that this book will be a great resource to you, that these chapters will help you to hold on and gain strength to persevere.

God has a plan that includes your success and happiness. God is moved by your faith. Since faith pleases God, allow these Points of Power to increase your faith. Whenever you feel the need, revisit the chapters that most encourage you! Remember: you have benefits and privileges as a child of God, so don't settle for mediocrity. You do have the power to change your life, your attitude, and your outlook.

In writing this book, I had so much available material that I had to choose my contents carefully. This is a very concise summary. Ladies and gentlemen, here are *your* Points of Power.

Yolanda
Adams

Chapter One

THE POWER OF FAITH

"I never dreamed of leaving the school system,"
she told the Billboard audience, "and when I did
it was a huge step, but I'm so glad I took that step
on faith. Now, my faith is to the point where it's
like, 'Give me a diving board over a pool with
no water, and watch me jump.'"

—*Yolanda*[1]

Faith Is How I Live

It is a foundation of trust in God at work in my life.

Life is beautiful. I remind myself of this fact every day. I'm optimistic. I don't complain because I live an amazing life. I live a life of expectation. I expect to be happy. I expect to be successful. I expect to make someone smile. But more than anything, I expect God's best for my life. I thank God for all I have every day.

Can you think of any times you've found yourself in a bad situation because you didn't exercise your faith in God? There certainly have been times in my life when I have moved ahead of God, only to wind up doing things God's way in the end.

I don't spend as much time asking God "Why?" as I once did. If I find myself in a challenging situation, my first inclination is to believe God. Knowing the Word of God is imperative! Every promise is God-breathed. Every promise removes doubt. Every promise builds faith. The Lord knows your destiny and knows your ability to reach your destination. With the support of a continually merciful God, you can move faithfully ahead no matter what you face.

I am the happiest person on earth when I totally rely on God.

Jesus tells us to have faith! For with faith, you have to wait on and trust in God's best for you.

The life God has prepared for us is so much better than our highest dreams. Just look at my life: I started off simply singing in a choir and spending my weekdays as a teacher. Then one day, God told me to quit. I stepped out in faith, left the classroom, and pursued my dreams. My music career is much more than I expected; I host a radio show and travel the world singing. Through my music, I am able to help strangers, friends, and family. God has shown me clearly in my life what He is willing to show you in yours: you never have to worry about reaching your destiny, because it's assured by your faith in God.

Abram was seventy-five years old when he received his promise from God: "Leave your country, your people and your father's household and go to the land I will show you. I will make you into a great nation and I will bless you" (Genesis 12:1–2 NIV).

It was a big request. God wanted Abram to uproot his life, leave everything that was familiar, and take his family into the unknown. And while it was impossible for Abram to know how God would deliver the promise, he believed the Lord would. He left home with his wife, Sarai, and his nephew Lot and set out for Canaan.

Looking back on the story of Abram and Sarai, I see them as two of the greatest icons of faith. They took God's words to heart, and the Lord delivered the covenant. And while they were remarkable people who walked the path of the Lord, it's important to remember that they were human beings, flawed and faltering like all of us. Abram's and Sarai's faith was by no means perfect, but rather something that evolved as the couple experienced great moments of weakness, insecurity, and impatience.

On the way to Canaan, they experienced one of their first

major trials, but instead of resting in faith, they moved forward in fear. The land they were traveling through was experiencing a great famine, and they knew they had to go to Egypt for survival. Before they entered, however, Abram grew worried. Sarai was very beautiful, and he thought if the Egyptians knew she was his wife, they would kill him and spare her. Not trusting in God to protect them and fulfill the Holy Spirit's promise, Abram and Sarai decided to lie. When asked who they were, Sarai responded that she was Abram's sister.

As expected, word of Sarai's beauty quickly circulated and Pharaoh, believing she was a single woman, took her as his wife. Soon after, however, the Lord sent numerous diseases to inflict Pharaoh and those in his household. Discovering the source of the plagues, Pharaoh summoned Abram and asked why he would do such a thing. He gave Sarai back and sent them out of Egypt.

The trial in Egypt was not the only one they encountered and not the only time they faltered. Their faith in God's timing was once again tested in Canaan, their new home. Abram and Sarai waited for fulfillment of God's promise that they would have children. They were growing worried. Both were now getting much older, and Sarai had yet to bear any children. She would soon be barren if she was not already, and the only heir Abram had was a servant named Eliezer.

Many years after asking Abram to leave his home, the Lord assured Abram He hadn't forgotten him and once again renewed His promise that Abram's descendants would outnumber the stars. But despite their belief in God, their faith slackened and they grew impatient.

After ten years of living in Canaan, Sarai began to think God intended to give Abram his heir through someone else, so she offered her maidservant Hagar. "Perhaps I can build a family through her," she said. But soon after Abram slept with Hagar and she conceived, Sarai was left feeling inadequate and abandoned. She had not trusted in God's plan, and she was now left with the unbearable knowledge that another woman was carrying her husband's child. In her grief, she mistreated Hagar and caused her to flee. Only after an angel of the Lord spoke with Hagar did she return to them to bear Abram's son, Ishmael. The impatience of Sarai and Abram brought grief upon their house, hurt the life of another, and brought them no closer to their goal of having a child of their own. They still had to wait on the promise of God and trust in His timing.

Thirteen years after the birth of Ishmael, when Abram was ninety-nine, the Lord once again cemented His covenant with Abram. He changed Abram's name to Abraham and Sarai's name to Sarah and promised that she would give birth to a son not a year later. Overhearing the promise, Sarah, who was then ninety, laughed. "After I am worn out and my master is old, will I now have this pleasure?" (Genesis 18:12 NIV). And yet, despite the inconceivable, the Lord fulfilled His promise. At the age of ninety, she gave birth to Isaac and made true the covenant of the Lord.

Power Passage

We live by faith, not by sight. (2 Corinthians 5:7 NIV)

Point of Practice

The point of power "Faith Is How I Live" is perfectly illustrated in the story of Abraham and Sarah. It is a beautiful account of human fault meeting God's perfection. It's important to remember we are imperfect beings with imperfect responses. Our faith is mixed with doubt. Just as Abraham and Sarah faltered, we too will falter, but God never gives up on us. On a daily basis I renew my trust in God, and He fulfills even the most implausible of promises.

You already have all you need to live by faith. Hebrews 11:8–10 reads,

> By faith Abraham, when called to go to a place he would later receive as his inheritance, obeyed and went, even though he did not know where he was going. By faith he made his home in the promised land like a stranger in a foreign country; he lived in tents, as did Isaac and Jacob, who were heirs with him of the same promise. For he was looking forward to the city with foundations, whose architect and builder is God. (NIV)

Over the years, I have learned that the longer you walk with God, the more your faith increases. I have put into practice the point of power "Faith Is How I Live" on a daily basis since I was a child. I begin and end my day with God in prayer. I talk to the Lord about what I have to do that day and ask to be a reflection of God's Spirit in every encounter I have and everything I do. I take stock of all my blessings and cultivate a heart of gratitude, giving thanks each morning and evening for all the good in my life. I leave anything that might trouble me with the Lord, because I know that no matter what obstacles I face, faith tells me that God has already cleared my path.

Point of Prayer

God, because of Your omniscience, You know eventually I will receive the revelation of Your presence. In Your presence, my faith is built. Confidence and courage are also restored when I realize, God, that You have me in Your hands. God, You are faithful and always keep Your promises!

10 Pensive Points

Reflect on the power of God's words. They come alive when we apply His truths and put them into action. Set aside time to do the activities and answer the questions below, and see the power of faith in your life!

1. Today, show that faith is important to you by doing a few simple things that are rooted in trust.

2. What is one important way your life relates to the story of Abraham and Sarah?

3. In your most recent challenging situation, did you trust in God's timing or did you take matters into your own hands?

4. What person in your life most hinders you from believing the promises of God?

5. What is one simple step you can take to live a life of faith?

6. It's easier to trust God in some areas of your life. What makes those areas in which it is harder to trust God so different?

7. What is the "promised land" God is calling you to? Take a long walk today and commit to listen to Him and follow His words.

8. As with Abraham and Sarah, your faith grows and becomes most evident when put to the test. Remember trials in your life that have tested your faith and recall how you persevered.

9. Remember the difficult times in your life when you felt abandoned or helpless, and how God provided for you when you couldn't see any way out.

10. Consider your family and friends who are walking in faith and note how their trust in God is impacting their lives.

Power Passage

In the gospel a righteousness from God is revealed, a righteousness that is by faith from first to last, just as it is written: "The righteous will live by faith." (Romans 1:17 NIV)

Faith Helps Me Find Rest

It's my way of finding inner peace.

It's the weekend. Hallelujah!" Have you ever spoken those words? Finally, at least two days of rest. If you're like me, though, you tend to fill those days with so much activity that you forget they're supposed to be there to give you rest. We treat God the same way. We try to tackle things on our own. We strive to be so self-reliant and independent that we carry baggage that isn't even ours. We forget that we have God—a place of complete rest!

We Christians are to think opposite of the ways folks normally do. When I'm weak, I'm really strong. When I'm sick, I'm really healed. It's what Joyce Meyer calls the "Upside-down Kingdom" mentality.

God never expects us to do anything alone. The Holy Spirit turns every tragedy into a triumph when we abide in the Lord. It's just like the old Christian hymn says: "Who, like Thyself, my guide and stay can be? Through cloud and sunshine, Lord, abide with me."[1] Resting in God and having faith that a higher power is in control allows us to set down our burdens and rest, to see the sunshine. For those who believe and have faith, God can bring an amazing sense of inner peace to even the most difficult trials.

Those who truly trust and depend on God for all things receive an anointing. People who don't abide in this realm of confidence can't possibly believe that anyone can live in such peace. I have been through a lot in my life. I know that I learn something from everything I endure. I also learn something from everyone I encounter. But I've never thought of my trials or circumstances as tools for God to get me back for something I did or did not do!

God is a loving, joyful, forgiving God. Use your faith and prayer to connect with the Holy Spirit, and no matter what, you will overcome. Take one day at a time. Work on your heart and spirit. Cry when you have to, but laugh more than you cry! Surround yourself with people who love you so much they won't let you give up! Approach every day expecting God's goodness, joy, and comfort.

Power Passage

Come to me, all you who are weary and burdened, and I will give you rest. (Matthew 11:28 NIV)

Point of Practice

One of the hardest things to admit in life is that we can't do things on our own all the time. We need support not only from our family and friends but, most of all, from God. When things get busy and complicated, sometimes we bite off more than we can chew. We try to answer questions we can never solve and load more on our backs than we can carry.

In these moments when we take our focus off the Holy Spirit and realize we don't have the answers, all we have to do to reconnect with God is to admit what was true all along: we don't have to do it alone. We can rest knowing the Lord is always walking before us, beside us, and behind us. God will lift us up anytime we call on the Lord.

Point of Prayer

God, You are my refuge. No matter what situation I am in, I only need to remind myself of Your glory and power and have faith that I am never alone. I can decide at any time to call on Your strength and summon the courage to listen to Your voice. I put my trust in You, Lord, to order my steps according to Your will as I walk with You and grow in faith of Your never-ceasing goodness and love.

10 Pensive Points

Put aside a few minutes today to sit quietly and think about some of the challenges you are currently facing. If your immediate response is "I don't have time to do that," that is your first clue you might be trying to do too much on your own. Are there any burdens you might need some help with? Are there ways God can help?

1. List one or more times in your life when you have felt abandoned or overwhelmed.
2. Did you or did you not respond by resting in God? Where did you look for help in your moment of crisis?
3. In difficult times, do you tend to rely on yourself, on others, or on God?
4. Is it difficult or easy for you to rely on God or others? Why?
5. Where do you feel most at rest?
6. Name one stereotype in your life that you have overcome.
7. When was the time you felt most completely alone?

8. When do you most distinctly feel God's presence?

9. What can you learn from how your friends cope in moments of difficulty?

10. What is one thing you can do to remain in God's rest throughout stormy waters?

Power Passage

You will keep in perfect peace
    him whose mind is steadfast,
    because he trusts in you. (Isaiah 26:3 NIV)

Faith Assures Me the Promises of God

It's my way of tapping into what is already mine.

Life is full. Our careers. Our relationships. Our talents. Our families. If you're like me, you plan things down to the tiniest detail and believe you know how your life should go. If you could have seen me as an awkward teenager, over six feet tall and very thin, you probably would have thought I'd be destined to a life spent playing basketball—certainly not singing!

I've learned we rarely look like the destiny inside us. I purposely played tennis because I hated the stereotype placed upon me by well-meaning onlookers. God had things other than sports planned for my future. Thank God for my parents and grandparents, who spoke faith words into me! Faith in God allows us to tap into our true destinies.

Even if we construct our own pretty life maps with neat roadside attractions and flag-waving finales, the Holy Spirit has greater plans for us. Faith in God allows us to tap into our true destinies and realize what is already ours. After a while, we realize it was in us all the time.

When I was teaching elementary school during the week and singing on the weekends I never imagined how much my life would eventually change. I loved being a teacher and working with the kids, but I started having trouble getting back to Houston in time to report to school Monday morning. I wanted to sing full-time, but I worried about giving up my steady teaching salary. How would I pay my bills on a singer's sporadic paycheck?

Still, because God had always taken care of me in the past, I knew I could stand in my faith. Why would the Lord abandon me now? I stepped out and quit my teaching job without having any idea what would happen, but knowing that God would support me. I've been singing ever since.

The following story of trusting an unexpected course can be instructive as we start realizing our biggest dreams. Throughout the Old Testament, the Israelites experienced bouts of faith and endured bouts of disbelief. With the swinging pendulum of their confidence, they fell in and out of favor with the Lord.

After being delivered from Egypt and slavery, the Israelites lost sight of what God had done for them and fell again into immorality. As a result, for seven years the Lord handed them over to the Midianites, people who destroyed everything the Israelites worked hard for—leveling their crops, slaughtering their cattle, and murdering any living thing in their way.

Living in fear, the Israelites crept into hiding. Instead of looking to the Lord for shelter, they found pockets in the mountains and hid out. They prayed meekly for deliverance but adapted the lifestyle of cowards.

Despite the Israelites' meek ways, the Lord was always with them. He sent Gideon, a prophet, a common young man from the tribe of Manasseh, to free the people of Israel and to condemn their worship of idols.

Gideon was an unlikely hero. He was from the weakest clan of Israel and was the smallest in his family. When an angel of the Lord found him and appeared to him, Gideon, like the other Israelites, was hiding out from the Midianites. The angel said to him, "The LORD is with you, mighty warrior" (Judges 6:12 NIV).

God didn't see Gideon as he was, but as he could be. The Lord said to him, "Go in the strength you have and save Israel out of Midian's hand. Am I not sending you? . . . I will be with you, and you will strike down all the Midianites together" (Judges 6:14, 16 NIV).

Gideon had his doubts. He was very unsure of both himself and God's command. He was a believer in the Lord, but he was also all too aware of his own inadequacies. He asked to see miracles as proof of God's will and signs that he truly had the Holy Spirit's blessing. Only then would he undertake what seemed to be an impossible mission.

As the battle approached, the odds against Gideon seemed to increase. His army that started with twenty-two thousand men dwindled to ten thousand. From there, the Lord decreased the army even further, refining the final cast of soldiers to only three hundred men.

But Gideon believed and God was faithful. In the middle of the night, Gideon and his army of three hundred approached the Midianite camp. At Gideon's sign, his men all blew their trumpets, broke their jars, and thrust their torches into the air. The Midianites were so confused that they turned their swords on one another, and the Lord delivered the land back into the hands of Israel.

Power Passage

If you have faith as small as a mustard seed, you can say to this mulberry tree, "Be uprooted and planted in the sea," and it will obey you. (Luke 17:6 NIV)

Point of Practice

Gideon was in hiding when God came to him. He was stowing away his wheat where the Midianites couldn't find it. But instead of calling him a coward, God called him a mighty warrior. He chose to see Gideon for who he could be rather than who he was.

God looks at us and sees our great potential. It doesn't matter what our disadvantages or weaknesses, the power of the Lord is enough to overcome any of our inherent obstacles.

The biggest challenge for Gideon wasn't fighting the battle. It was *believing* that he could win. Evaluate your own life. What are your weaknesses? What do you believe about your inabilities? What do you consider impossible?

Faith assures the promises of God. God is with you daily. Just as He helped Gideon defeat the numerous Midianites with only three hundred men, He will help you conquer your obstacles with the strength you have.

Point of Prayer

God, I pray in faith, knowing that You are real. You are a loving, supportive God who is with me all the time. I go about my day in my work, my relationships with people, and the many other parts of my life knowing that You care about me, that You are listening to me, and that You are guiding me in all I do. I hold fast to my faith and rely on the strength I have in You in all things.

10 Pensive Points

We are happy for our friends and loved ones when they overcome challenges or enjoy a great achievement, but when it comes to ourselves, like Gideon, sometimes we wonder if those good things are for "other people." Are there reasons you don't believe you are good enough for God's blessing? Take a few minutes to think about this question: Are you blocking God's blessings in your life?

1. In what one way does Gideon's faith resemble yours?

2. In what one way does Gideon's faith differ from yours?

3. How are the people of Israel a symbol for your faith life?

4. Make a list of your biggest weaknesses.

5. Think of one way you would be considered the underdog.

6. Think back to a seemingly "impossible" thing you were able to accomplish.

7. Remember what it took for you to get to that point of victory.

8. Consider the role faith played in your success.

9. What are the common qualities of the unlikely heroes in your life?

10. Meditate on one way you can refine your faith to live more like Gideon.

Power Passage

The promise comes by faith, so that it may be by grace and may be guaranteed to all Abraham's offspring—not only to those who are of the law but also to those who are of the faith of Abraham. (Romans 4:16 NIV)

Faith Helps Me Overcome

I stand firm in faith.

We've all been there. We've experienced those moments when our knees fall to the ground and we think we'll never be able to get back up. We think a situation is so big, a problem so large, that absolutely nothing can beat it. Have you ever thought a situation was so challenging that you couldn't overcome it? Or have you ever had a dream that seemed so outlandish that you thought it was impossible to achieve?

Well, the truth is, sometimes things are impossible for *us*. That's where faith in God comes in. No matter what's too big for *you*, it's never too big for the Almighty. God's plan is so purposeful that down the road we will see His sovereignty. Stand firm on the foundation of God's unfailing power. We might not understand it now, but He has weaved a divine plan with incomprehensible intricacy for you from the moment you are born. Faith in God is a solid rock. Stand firm, and it will always support you and enable you to come eye-to-eye with the impossible.

Consider my music career. People see me now and think I was some kind of overnight success, but nothing could be further from the truth. What they don't know is that I've been singing and walking with God for a very long time. From the very beginning of my career it has always been important to me that all kinds of people hear my music—not just typical gospel fans, but everybody.

God's Word is about faith, hope, and love. Who doesn't want to hear that? Why would I want to reserve the Lord's powerful message for only a select few? Yet, if you asked most people in the record industry, they would have said that gospel music is for "church people." The record industry executives see gospel music as a very distinct category; gospel artists rarely have their music played on mainstream radio stations.

It was never my goal to change the face of gospel music, but I have always worked to give God the just praise that is due Him in everything I accomplish in my life. I think the Lord is really cool and I want people to see that for themselves. So even though people wanted to keep me in a "gospel box," I stayed true to who I was and honored the music that I love. That includes gospel, but it also includes jazz, R & B, some rock, and even some hip-hop. As a result, I've certainly had my critics, people who have said that I am not a true gospel singer.

For me gospel music is not all about choir robes and shouting. Sure, that can be part of it and there's nothing wrong with that; but it's not all about that. Often when you see gospel music depicted in the movies, it's exclusively for the church. You have ladies with their hair done up high or wearing oversized hats of all colors of the rainbow. They are fainting and falling out into the aisles or fanning themselves with one hand and playing the tambourine with the other. But Sunday morning is about teaching; people come to church to learn the teachings of Jesus. They want something to take home with them that will help them get through the week. That's not a concern just for church people; that's something everybody wants.

If anyone needed proof that God's message is universal, all

they'd have to do is look at the record sales of songs like "Open My Heart." It became one of the most requested songs on R & B radio stations across the country. In the song I sing about those times when you feel as if your hopes and dreams will never come true and you just don't think you have the strength to keep going. No matter who you are, whether or not you have ever stepped foot inside a church, chances are you've had that feeling. Life can be hard, but then comes the good news: God is the One who can help you get through it. You just have to open your heart to the Lord's blessings.

Gospel's message is God's message. It shows you that good is in every situation, and that's a message people, no matter who they are, like to hear. People told me it was impossible to reach both secular and nonsecular audiences at the same time, but I think artists like me, and people who paved the way such as Kirk Franklin, Sounds of Blackness, Take 6, CeCe Winans, and John P. Kee, have proven them wrong. Nothing is impossible with God's help. Nothing is impossible with faith.

Coach Don Meyer is a man who knows something about the "impossible." There was a six-car caravan behind him when a semitruck sideswiped his car in South Dakota. His Toyota crossed the yellow lines, flipping into a ditch. He was pinned in his vehicle until the ambulance came. A head basketball coach for thirty-seven seasons, Meyer had been on his way to a preseason retreat. The entire Northern State team and his assistant coaches were behind him. It was one of those moments where death and life share a fine line and a matter of mere minutes can save years or take them away. While he sat pinned in his car, his team sat loyally beside him, keeping him awake. Finally help came and he was life-flighted to a hospital in Sioux Falls and taken immediately into surgery.

The accident was nearly fatal; Coach Meyer suffered numerous serious injuries. His left side sustained the brunt of the damage:

all his ribs were broken and his leg was completely crushed. Internal injuries were extensive. His spleen and part of his intestines were removed in surgery. But that wasn't all. While the doctors were trying to treat him for the injuries caused by the car crash, they found something unexpected: cancer.

Sometimes in life it's impossible to believe that things can get worse. With so much taken away, you wonder what you even have left to give. Fighting near-fatal injuries and a leg so severely damaged that it was eventually amputated, Meyer was told there was something new he'd have to fight.

It would have been easy to give up, yet he chose to see the accident as a blessing in disguise. In a statement read at a news conference, he said:

> It is now 10 a.m. on Friday, Sept. 12. My trauma surgeon, David Strand, just told me they found characinoid cancer in my liver and small bowels. The cancer was discovered during the emergency surgery after my wreck on Sept. 5. What's great about this is I would not have known about the cancer had I not had the wreck. God has blessed me with the one thing we all need, which is truth. I can now fight with all of my ability. What I now ask is that everybody who believes in God would praise Him for this discovery and pray to Him to give me the strength, patience and peace to be a man of God on this journey. I am looking forward to coaching this season and am forever thankful to my team who saved my life and the coaching staff who has stepped up to the plate.

Two months after the car crash, numerous surgeries later, and in the beginning stages of cancer treatment, Coach Meyer was once again on the road with his team. It was a new life, full of new difficulties and daily struggles, but also one of new blessings. Grounded in faith and the belief that God's vision is greater than his own, he proved himself to be off the court what he has always been on it: a great competitor.[1]

Power Passage

Be on your guard; stand firm in the faith; be men of courage; be strong. Do everything in love. (1 Corinthians 16:13–14 NIV)

Point of Practice

Aren't you grateful for God's Spirit? He gives us strength to persevere. Our trials and difficulties exist to build us up. God provides hope and endurance when we least expect it. Coach Meyer's story is one of great heartbreak and grief, but also of incredible courage and integrity. At the time of the wreck, it would have been easy to ask "Why me?" The natural instinct is self-pity and a feeling of injustice. Instead, Coach Meyer didn't ask why it happened, but how he could overcome it. He understands the essential lesson that God uses all situations for the good. Without the car crash, he might not have found his cancer in time, and he's come to appreciate the fact that the wreck that nearly took his life ended up being the very thing that saved it.

In life's difficult situations, don't look down in despair, but look up in hope. God is faithful to those who have faith in Him. As it is written in James 1:2–4: "Consider it pure joy, my brothers, whenever you face trials of many kinds, because you know that the testing of your faith develops perseverance. Perseverance must finish its work so that you may be mature and complete, not lacking anything" (NIV).

Point of Prayer

God, I know You always make a way. I know You are always there for me, and when I pray for Your guidance, You will show me the direction to go. When I walk steady in my faith in You, I know You will always deliver me to a better place.

10 Pensive Points

Think about the times things seemed impossible in your life. God is always with us no matter what the situation. All that is required of us is to call on the Lord, and in the Holy Spirit we get reacquainted with our God-given strength, clarity, and peace. Today, find some time to get quiet and invite God into a challenge you are facing.

1. How would you have responded if you were in Coach Meyer's position? Would you have been able to see the accident as a blessing?

2. Think of "accidents" in your life that have turned out to be blessings.

3. Our faith is most evident in the midst of challenges. Remember how you trusted during one of your life's obstacles.

4. What needs in your life do you feel are too big for God to meet?

5. List struggles you are finding hard to overcome right now.

6. For each listed item, what is one way you can rest in the faithfulness of God?

7. Think back to a situation in the past where God intervened and helped you overcome.

8. Remember times you have seen God work miracles in the lives of those you love.

9. Ask a trusted friend to help you see one way you can change your attitude to find hope in affliction.

10. Help another friend see God's mercy during a difficulty he or she is facing.

Power Passage

Everyone born of God overcomes the world. This is the victory that has overcome the world, even our faith. Who is it that overcomes the world? Only he who believes that Jesus is the Son of God. (1 John 5:4–5 NIV)

Chapter Two

THE POWER OF LOVE

"As a Christian, I want more than ever to show others the power of God's love. You don't do that by badgering people; you do it by being a good example."

—Yolanda, after the September 11, 2001, attacks on the World Trade Center in New York, the Pentagon in DC, and the crash of United Airlines Flight 93 in Shanksville, Pennsylvania[1]

God's Love Produces Joy and the Abundant Life

God's plan is always bigger and better.

Love, love, love. Is there anything more wonderful than love? We live for it. It determines our countenance. When we're in love, we dress differently and act differently. There's a twinkle in our eyes and pep in our steps.

God's love produces sweet joy.

While our plans for ourselves are big, God's plans are even bigger. If we truly want the abundant life, we cannot live in the tunnel of limited dreams.

The biggest truth about God's Word is that God is love and His love produces joy. When we allow ourselves to follow His footsteps and pursue His truths, when we forsake our plans for the glories He has promised, we will know joy in the purest and most beautiful sense and we will have the abundant life.

I love to sing. I cannot describe the intense feeling of joy I experience when I perform or when people approach me or write to me to say that one of my songs has touched their life in some way.

I was four years old when I sang my first solo in church, "Jesus

Loves Me." I grew up in a musical household. My parents both had great voices, as do all my siblings. We listened to all kinds of music, not just gospel. Everything from jazz and blues to classical and country and western was played in my house. Singing is what I believe to be my God-given purpose. I write songs and sing because I want people to know that God is present in our lives every moment of every single day. The Lord's goodness and presence are always with us.

If I hadn't followed God's message to leave my teaching career, had I not listened to the Lord's voice and pursued singing, I don't know where my life would be right now. God is always speaking to us, offering us guidance about which option to choose or which direction to take. Singing brought me such profound, indescribable joy that I've always known it was a gift from God. Since the day I found the courage to follow my love of music, to pursue it wholeheartedly, I've been rewarded beyond my wildest dreams.

My experience with music is very similar to the story of Solomon in the Bible. Solomon was young when he became king of the Hebrews. The son of David, he knew just how tremendous the task was that lay before him. The people in his kingdom were great and the stretch of his power was wide, and not just anyone could rule such a vast kingdom well. He worried about the inadequacies of his own youth and inexperience, but he was far more prepared for the task than he imagined.

One night in a dream, God approached Solomon and asked the new king what he wanted. Solomon's answer was not typical. He did not ask for riches or fame. He did not ask for good looks or women. Instead, he asked for the most valuable thing of all: wisdom.

O LORD my God, you have made your servant king in place of my father David. But I am only a little child and do not know how to carry out my duties. Your servant is here among the people you have chosen, a great people, too numerous to count or number. So give your servant a discerning heart to govern your people and to distinguish between right and wrong. For who is able to govern this great people of yours? (1 Kings 3:7–9 NIV)

Because of his humble and selfless request, God blessed Solomon, promising him an abundant life. And not only did He impart wisdom to the new king, He blessed him tenfold: "I will give you a wise and discerning heart, so that there will never have been anyone like you, nor will there ever be. Moreover, I will give you what you have not asked for—both riches and honor—so that in your lifetime you will have no equal among kings" (1 Kings 3:12–13 NIV).

From the start of his reign with the blessing of the Lord, Solomon's wisdom echoed throughout the kingdom. People from far and wide sought his advice on matters dearest to their hearts.

Perhaps the most famous case of Solomon's guidance involved two prostitutes and their babies. Both women lived in the same household and gave birth to sons within the same week. One night, shortly after the babies were born, one of them died. The mother of the dead boy switched the babies, taking the live one for her own. In the morning, when the other mother awoke, she was horrified to find her baby dead beside her. When she looked closer, she discovered that the boy was not her own. The two women began to fight over the living boy and took their case to King Solomon.

In his God-given wisdom, Solomon knew the love of a mother was one of the greatest loves of all. He asked a servant to bring him a sword and told the women his verdict: he would chop the living child in half, giving one part to each mother.

While one of the women accepted his verdict, the other begged for mercy, asking Solomon to spare the child and give it to the other woman. Seeing such true compassion and love for the boy, Solomon knew the baby was hers and gave him back to her. The woman's overflowing love caused the return of her most prized possession.

This story of Solomon and his wisdom tells the true love of a mother who was willing to lose her child rather than see him die. God's love is greater than this love. It absolutely is.

Power Passage

Delight yourself in the LORD
> and he will give you the desires of your heart.
> (Psalm 37:4 NIV)

Point of Practice

The story of Solomon's wisdom stands as a great symbol for our prayer lives—what we should ask for and how we should ask for it. The natural instinct is to ask for what we most deeply desire. Many times when I've prayed, I've pleaded, "Lord, please help me keep my job; help me stay in this relationship; help me make the mortgage payment this month." The list goes on.

Our view of our destinies is limited. We sometimes have difficulty seeing beyond our present circumstances and pains. But God sees the whole picture. He sees how the story is going to unfold and the best way to get us there. Solomon's request for wisdom was a faith-filled request. He trusted that the Lord's plans were bigger than his own, and he simply wanted discerning eyes and ears to do what he was supposed to do.

Point of Prayer

God, I know that Your plans for me are bigger than anything I can imagine for myself. Guide me, Lord, and help me to look for the good You promise me every day and in everything.

10 Pensive Points

Read the story of Solomon again in 1 Kings 3. Find a place to sit quietly and consider all God has already manifested in your life. Look beyond your own dreams and desires to the abundant life God has waiting for you.

1. What would you have asked for if the Lord promised you one request?
2. Spend time this week reading 1 Kings. Envision Solomon living out the dream of the abundant life.
3. Jot down in a journal the big plan for your life.
4. Consider whether it is your plan or the Lord's.
5. Where is God leading you that you're not willing to go?
6. In what area in your life do you see the greatest need for God's gift of wisdom and God's guidance?
7. Think about the story of the two prostitutes. Which one most represents you?
8. Name one thing you would be willing to sacrifice everything for.
9. Who sacrificed everything for you? How can you live that truth more honestly?
10. Think of three ways you can realize the abundant life through acts of selfless giving.

Power Passage

Let all who take refuge in you be glad;
    let them ever sing for joy.
Spread your protection over them,
    that those who love your name may rejoice
    in you. (Psalm 5:11 NIV)

God's Love Makes Me More Than a Conqueror

I am a warrior of the heart.

The ability to love another is God's greatest gift to us. It's wonderful to love. Our hearts and feelings are our dearest God-given possessions. Songs are written about love, movies honor love, and a holiday celebrates it. We all love to love, but the truth is our hearts are fragile, and when they break, they sometimes take a long time to recover. Our hearts remember our pains. As we grow and mature, we learn to be less careless with our hearts, to honor and protect them as the special gifts they are, but it's nearly impossible to keep hearts from getting hurt no matter how hard we try.

I have been so blessed to have so much love in my life! I can't say it enough. I have a wonderful family, amazing friends, and my wonderful little daughter, Taylor Ayana, whom I love more than I ever imagined I could love anyone or anything. Still, God does not promise us lives without hurt. Despite all my wonderful blessings, I experienced a profound loss of love at an early age with the death of my father. And while the loss of his presence in our daily lives was a severe pain, I learned something remarkable about God's true love.

My dad, Major Adams, was my hero. He was a track star in college. He was even inducted into the Drake Hall of Fame. I learned perseverance and determination from him. I developed my love for running and golf from him. He was not a perfect man, but he was a great man. Every little girl thinks her father is Superman, and I was no exception.

As the result of a horrific car crash, my dad was airlifted to Ben Taub Hospital in Houston, Texas. He was in a coma for four months. It was pretty hard on the family because my mom was at the hospital every day. The younger children didn't understand; they just knew Dad wasn't home. He was an active father. He played and wrestled with the boys every night before bed. To not have him there made the house seem empty.

A few months before his accident, he sat down with me and started explaining insurance policies, checkbook balancing, and money management. I recall asking him why he was doing this, and his reply was, "You're the oldest, and you need to know it in case something happens to me and your mom." A few months later it did.

The day my dad passed, he first woke up briefly from his coma. He looked good! He couldn't really speak because of the tube in his throat, but I asked him if he was okay, and he nodded his head. Then I asked him if he would be coming home with us, and he fiercely shook his head no. Of course this shook me. My hero, my dad whom I loved so much, said he was okay but wouldn't be coming home. He knew he was going to see the Father, a Father who loved him so much that He wouldn't let him suffer another day.

Power Passage

Above all else, guard your heart,
for it is the wellspring of life.
(Proverbs 4:23 NIV)

Point of Practice

Knowing the unconditional love of God, we have to accept that God knows best. One of my immature questions to God was "*Why my* dad, Lord?" God replied, "Because your dad would never have been satisfied being hooked up to tubes and machines for the rest of his life!" From that day on, I have trusted that what God allows is best. I often wonder: If Dad had lived, would I be as determined and headstrong as I am now? I doubt it.

Through the experience of my father's death, I learned that it is in life's moments of pain and hurt that our faith is tested most and, in turn, where we can grow the most. God asks us to lay down our fears, resentments, questions, and pains and come to Him in a place of hope. In Matthew 11:28 He says, "Come to me, all you who are weary and burdened, and I will give you rest" (NIV).

When you face tragedy and pain, allow yourself to grieve. You can never reach a place of healing without first allowing yourself to reach a place of hurt. But in the midst of your sadness, do not wallow. Look to the Lord for strength and understanding, and He will move you forward, day by day, to a place of restoration. Through Him, you will become a warrior of the heart.

Point of Prayer

God, I may not always understand why things are as they are, but I understand that it is not for me to know. It is all a part of Your plan for me. Help me to live in Your light, God, and place my trust in You. Help me to know that wherever You take me is where I am supposed to go.

10 Pensive Points

Love is God's greatest gift. But our hearts are fragile. God knows all your feelings and hurts. Resting in the Lord's never-ceasing love can bring you peace. Take a little time to consider the love in your life. Are there pains you need to let God help you with?

1. Reflect on what it means to you to be a "warrior of the heart."

2. Have you experienced the loss of a loved one? Write down your own experience, using the story about my father as a model.

3. Note similarities and differences between your story and my story.

4. Think of one area of your life where you have to persevere through emotional pain.

5. Think back on how you reacted to the loss of a family member, and ways you coped.

6. When tragedy occurs, what one concrete action shows that you allow yourself to be engulfed in pain? What one concrete action shows that you look for the hand of the Lord in all circumstances?

7. Think of someone you know who learned to find faith amid his or her grief. What can you learn from that person about grief *with hope*?

8. Focus on an unexpected good in your life, and then trace it back to a past tragedy that was part of the pathway for that benefit.

9. How has pain in your life been of use in the lives of others?

10. Identify three friends or family members who are enduring difficult times and whom you can help.

Power Passage

In all these things we are more than conquerors through him who loved us. (Romans 8:37 NIV)

God Loved Me Even Before
I Knew Him

God's love is inherent love.

We live in a culture where people have perfected the art of putting their best foot forward. We strive to make great first impressions by dressing well, smiling wide, and displaying our most charming behavior. We want people to like us. We change and improve to make others like us more.

I am no different. Everyone knows that I love fashion. I modeled as a teenager. Just as I love to mix things up in my music, I also love to make out-of-the-gospel-box choices in the clothes I wear onstage. The young people especially appreciate that I don't dress like the typical gospel singer in sequins. I love to wear beautiful, sophisticated couture outfits when I perform.

Still, as much as I enjoy wearing beautiful clothes, I know it has nothing to do with who I am as a person, as a child of God. It's just part of being an entertainer. Dressing a certain way for a concert or a photo shoot is important, but in life, God's love always sees us with our best foot forward. The Lord's love doesn't demand designer clothes, witty banter, perfect manners, or brilliant intellect. God loved us even before we knew Him, and there's absolutely nothing we can do to increase or diminish God's already overflowing love for us.

Most young girls have at some point dreamed of being ballerinas with thin, tiny physiques wrapped in pink tutus and graceful lines. In their dreams, they see themselves floating across the stage, twirling and being lifted high in the air by a handsome partner. It's the perfect image of a princess.

In the real life of a ballerina, beauty doesn't come easily. As the girls in their tights and shoes grow older and get better, the demand on their physiques increases. Being a ballerina means being fragilely thin.

Kirsten Haglund was one of those girls. She diligently pursued her dream of life as a professional ballerina. The pursuit was devastating for her. She couldn't find the healthy line between being fit and being unhealthy. She slipped into anorexia. She became fixated on her weight and saw her slender frame as too big and imperfect. It wasn't until her parents intervened that she recognized the problem, made her own decision to recover, and decided to remove herself from the art form she dearly loved. She knew she couldn't pursue a career that rewarded a dangerous idea of being extremely thin.

Since getting help and moving forward, Kirsten Haglund has found a new face for beauty. Crowned Miss America in 2008, the nineteen-year-old, five-foot-eight-inch blonde has taken the opportunity afforded her by the crown to talk to teens across America about the importance of a healthy body image. More than seventy million people in the world struggle with eating disorders. Nearly 40 percent of anorexia cases are found in girls ages fifteen to nineteen.

Now in recovery from her battle with anorexia, Kirsten still struggles with food choices. Talking to others about her illness and recovery helps her heal and stay focused on being healthy. It is important to her to give to others and show them that everyone has some kind of challenge to overcome. Part of her recovery is learning to cope with her illness and to be strong, but without God's love she knows she couldn't have done it. By sharing her struggle to love the beauty God gave her and accept her body as it is, she hopes to show other young women with eating disorders that recovery is possible.[1]

Power Passage

I am convinced that neither death nor life, neither angels nor demons, neither the present nor the future, nor any powers, neither height nor depth, nor anything else in all creation, will be able to separate us from the love of God that is in Christ Jesus our Lord. (Romans 8:38–39 NIV)

Point of Practice

We desire to be the best. We believe there are ways we can "fix" ourselves—become more beautiful, more lovable, more accepted. Think about your own life. How many times have you thought you would finally look the way you wanted if you could just lose those ten pounds? How often have you paid a heavy handful of cash for a high-end haircut or designer brand because you thought a new style could create a "new and better" you?

Self-love is the hardest love for some people to achieve. We see the airbrushed photos of superstars who look as if they don't have any physical flaws. The reality is even they don't look like their images on movie posters and in magazines.

While it's hard for us to believe, the truth is we can't come to the table with more than who we already are. Jeremiah 1:5 states:

"Before I formed you in the womb I knew you, before you were born I set you apart" (NIV).

We are the templates of the Holy Spirit! This tells me if God loves us enough to place Himself inside us, we must be pretty cool. No matter what you encounter, loving yourself is important. Love your hair, love your skin, love your nose, and love your body enough to treat it well. Exercise, eat right, and drink lots of water. You'll be surprised at how great you feel!

In His love and in His divine creation, God created us to be the most beautiful version of ourselves. God has a dream for each of us individually, and He wants us to pursue those dreams whole-heartedly. But to pursue His dream, we have to abandon society's expectations. The standard that matters most is God's.

Point of Prayer

God, help me to see myself as You see me: a perfect creation made in Your image.

10 Pensive Points

Put aside a few minutes to get quiet inside, maybe go for a long walk or find a place where you can be alone for a while and consider how you see yourself. Reflect on God's words from Psalm 18:30: "As for God, his way is perfect; the word of the LORD is flawless. He is a shield for all who take refuge in him" (NIV). Are you constantly at war with yourself, always trying to change who you are? Or are you living your life as if you are one of God's perfect creations made in His image?

1. Think back on your own self-image as a teen. Is there anything in your memory that helps you sympathize with Kirsten Haglund's struggle?

2. Find your favorite photo of yourself and use it to point out the parts of yourself you are unsatisfied with.

3. When you think of yourself, do you think first of the internal or the external?

4. Write down your role models for beauty—inside and out. Next to each name, list that person's most prominent characteristics.

5. Who are two others you know who struggle with their body image?

6. What one thing can you do to help them realize their own beauty?

7. What do you do that shows you believe God loves you just as you are?

8. Identify one thing you do or think that is stopping you from seeing yourself the way God sees you. Identify one thing others do or say that is stopping you from seeing yourself the way God sees you.

9. List three people or activities that encourage your walk toward a healthy acceptance of yourself.

10. Think of one bodacious way you can begin a transformation from self-acceptance to celebration of the you God created and loves.

Power Passage

We love because he first loved us. (1 John 4:19 NIV)

God's Love Cleanses Me

I have a new beginning.

I love to go to spas and indulge in their services. I have made it my mission to visit every spa in North and South America! I've enjoyed the Miami Mandarin and Westin Diplomat. I love manicures and pedicures, wraps and scrubs, and long aromatherapy massages. Spending time in a beautiful, peaceful spa, with the soft music playing, the slow deliberate pace and hushed voices, sitting in my fluffy robe and slippers, sipping elixirs and herbal teas, is like being a world away. Giving myself the gift of a little pampering and relaxation makes me feel rejuvenated and is an important part of my self-care regimen, as are prayer, a good healthy diet, and exercise.

One of my favorite treatments is the rainforest shower that covers your entire body with sprays of pure, fresh water. I close my eyes and imagine the water flow as God cleansing me with His love. It's the ultimate cleansing.

Most of us, when looking over our pasts, have at least a few things we've done that we are ashamed of. Even those of us who seem to have things completely together admit we've had a few dark moments. When we are being especially hard on ourselves and are replaying the tape of regrets and sins in our minds, we wonder if we will ever be good enough to be loved.

The power of God's love is not only in forgiveness, but also in God's cleansing. God doesn't just give us back our old lives, the Lord hands us brand-new ones, pardoning even our darkest sins. God cleanses every sin and forgives every wrong. I love Him for that. And the amazing thing is that this cleansing is available to everyone, no matter who you are, no matter what you've done. Think about that. It's available to *everyone*. Even people like Rahab.

Jericho was full of many people: Teachers. Priests. Artists. Lawyers. Businessmen. Fathers. Mothers. With so many inside the walls, one has to wonder why God reached out and found His hero in a harlot, why He picked through those who were honest and forthright and chose Rahab.

Rahab's story begins with Joshua. In the process of conquering the promised land, Joshua and his army came across Jericho. Knowing he would attack the city in the days ahead, he sent two spies in to get a better lay of the land. When they entered Jericho, the two spies sought refuge in Rahab's house. Aware that the Israelites were in the area, Jericho's king found out about the two men and sent guards to Rahab's house to arrest them. But Rahab had a different plan in mind. She had heard about the God of Israel, His miracles and His mercy. Despite her ungodly ways, in her heart she believed in the strength and promises of the Lord, and she decided to protect the two spies. She risked her life and told the king's guards that the two men had left and they should hurry to catch them.

Having given the king's guards wrong information, she returned to Joshua's spies and promised to protect them if they protected her and her family in the coming attack. "I know that the LORD has given this land to you and that a great fear of you has fallen on us, so that all who live in this country are melting in fear because of you," she said (Joshua 2:9 NIV). "Now then, please swear to me by the LORD that you will show kindness to my family, because I have shown kindness to you" (2:12 NIV). Seeing her belief and sincerity, the spies promised to spare her home. In return, she helped them escape from the city by way of a scarlet rope. After they left, she kept the rope hanging as a sign for the Israelites to remember that hers was the house that belonged to the Lord.

Because of her faith and dedication, when the city of Jericho fell, Rahab and her family were spared. Her old ways and sinful past were of no consequence to the Lord because she knew in her heart and spoke with her mouth that God was the Ruler of all.

Power Passage

Love is patient, love is kind. It does not envy, it does not boast, it is not proud. It is not rude, it is not self-seeking, it is not easily angered, it keeps no record of wrongs. Love does not delight in evil but rejoices with the truth. It always protects, always trusts, always hopes, always perseveres. (1 Corinthians 13:4–7 NIV)

Point of Practice

God always uses unlikely heroes. From David to Zacchaeus to the good Samaritan, God rarely chooses the expected individual. Rahab is one of the most beautiful examples of God's great cleansing power and His ability to use the smallest and weakest to accomplish amazing things.

In Isaiah 1:18 it is written,

"Come now, let us reason together,"
says the LORD.

"Though your sins are like scarlet,
      they shall be as white as snow;
though they are red as crimson,
      they shall be like wool." (NIV)

God does not ask for perfection; He merely asks for our faith. If we are willing to trust in Him, not only will He grant us a good life, He will grant us the best life there is. As believers in God, we must find power in His cleansing love. Neither anything we have done nor anything we will ever do can separate us from His infinite grace if we believe. He bestowed such mercy and blessing on the life of Rahab; what will He bestow on you?

Point of Prayer

God, You are a forgiving God. Cleanse my heart and soul of sin and make me anew in Your love.

10 Pensive Points

We have all done things that we wished we hadn't. Maybe we've said something hurtful to someone else, or even to ourselves. Consider the people in your life. Have you done anything you now regret? Reflect on God's ability to forgive and cleanse us of our sins so that we have the power to start fresh at any moment.

1. For the next three days, note on your calendar one part of Rahab's story that you identify with.
2. Out of everyone in Jericho, why do you think God chose to save Rahab?
3. Think about your past. In what sin have you, like Rahab,

been immersed? What in your past seemed inescapable? Remember how you felt.

4. What regrets and sins do you still struggle with? Do you believe anything you've done is unforgivable?

5. List one active step you are taking to change.

6. What is one thing you find it hard to forgive in yourself?

7. Write these words in your journal or someplace where you can see them often: "I believe that I've truly been forgiven and that God has given me a brand-new start."

8. Think about your friends and family and focus on someone you know who has been able to transform his or her life through faith in Jesus Christ. How has God's love affected this person?

9. If you were given a clean slate today with your family, your friends, your job, your relationships, your civic record, and your dreams, think of one thing you would do.

10. What's stopping you from doing that right now?

Power Passage

You are already clean because of the word I have spoken to you. (John 15:3 NIV)

Chapter Three

THE POWER OF FORGIVENESS

"For the person who feels that Christians don't do anything wrong, they don't say anything wrong, they don't act wrong, that's not it—Christians are just forgiven."

—*Yolanda*[1]

Through God, I Am Given the Power to Forgive

I am a gracious imitator of God.

Forgiveness is one of the most powerful things you can do for yourself. Are you surprised to read the words "for *yourself*"? Many people make the mistake of thinking that forgiveness is about the persons who hurt them. They think, *Why should I forgive them? I don't want to do anything for them!* Forgiveness isn't about *them*, forgiveness is about *you*! There are few things in life more freeing or more liberating than forgiving someone else.

Part of our human nature is to feel entitled to justice and entitled to sadness. In our hurt, we go to extremes. We call things "unforgivable" and swear nothing could ever remedy the problem. We get caught up in the wrong we've been dealt; we walk around with heavy baggage we don't need to bear. To decide not to forgive is like remaining in prison after your bail has been paid, after you've served your time and the guards have come and opened the cell to set you free. God has given you the gift of freedom, but you would rather stay in chains, locked up and shackled to the person who hurt you, because you won't forgive. The surest way to stay stuck in unhappiness and misery is to walk in a state of unforgiveness.

Forgiveness is God's gift to us. Claim it! All we need to be set free of the burden and heaviness of a revengeful spirit is to forgive. None of us are without sin, but the gift of the Christian life is that when we fall down, by God's grace we have the ability to get up and start again.

At some point, we are all in need of forgiveness. The best way to keep moving forward in life is to forgive anyone who has hurt you. Start today. Don't waste any more time. If there are people you need to forgive, call them up, write them a letter, or simply decide to let go of the hurt; let go of having to be right or getting revenge, and move on. Most of the time the people who have hurt us don't even realize we are angry at them. They've gone on with their lives and aren't even thinking about us.

I know what some of you are thinking: *Yolanda, it is not that easy. You don't know what he or she did to me.* That is true; I don't know the particulars of your situation. What I do know is how bad I feel when I have been hurt and rather than let it go, rather than forgive as God has taught me, I stay attached to anger or unforgiveness. Life is too short to walk around feeling upset and weighted down. If you are focused on what is wrong, you can't see all the blessings the Holy Spirit has waiting for you. And in order to be forgiven, we must also forgive.

If you can't picture how forgiveness can change your life, think about the role it has played in the lives of some of the world's greatest civil rights leaders: Gandhi, Martin Luther King Jr., and, most recently, Nelson Mandela.

About five miles off the coast of Cape Town, South Africa, sits Robben Island. From 1960 to 1991, it was a jail for the country's apartheid regime, housing political prisoners and those most loyal to the cause of human freedom. Nelson Mandela served eighteen of his twenty-seven years of imprisonment there in a six-by-nine cell, calling Robben the "harshest, most iron-fisted outpost in the South African penal system."

During his years at Robben, Mandela saw plenty of heartache and brutality. Black prisoners were treated like animals. Sometimes for fun, the white guards would take prisoners out to the back to dig trenches. After hours of hard labor, they'd force them down in the dirt confines and urinate on the unlucky souls who were tired from digging.

On Robben, life was a continual parade of pain. The prisoners were allowed only two visitors a year, and their living conditions were abysmal. They worked in rock quarries, chipping away at heavy slabs of limestone, compressing the shards to powder, then hauling it long distances. It would have been heavy and hard work for even a healthy man, but it was debilitating for the prisoners who were already harshly treated and underfed. Yet Mandela maintained the poise of a studied diplomat, his compassion and kindness overreaching.

Mistreated though they were, the prisoners on Robben were believers in hope. Spurred on by the character of Mandela, they believed in the South Africa to come. They beat the limestone to powder to beat a system of suffering. In 1964, just before Mandela had been sentenced, he stood in the Pretoria courtroom and made the mandate he would live out during his years on the island: "During my lifetime...I have cherished the ideal of a democratic and free society in which all persons live together in harmony with equal opportunities, it is an ideal which I hope to live for and achieve," he said. "But if needs be, it is an ideal for which I am prepared to die."

Though it took decades, death, and pain, Mandela's ideal—and the ideal of thousands of other South Africans—was realized.

Years after he left Robben Island and the apartheid regime was dismantled, Mandela was elected South Africa's first official president. He invited those who had hurt him most to his inauguration banquet: Percy Yutar, the lawyer who had diligently worked for his execution: and P. W. Botha, the apartheid regime's leader. To his first dinner as president, Mandela invited the wardens of Robben Island, making clear what he had promised all along. The new South Africa did not hold on to its past. The new South Africa was the home of reconciliation and forgiveness.

"Men of peace," he said, "must not think about retribution or recriminations. Courageous people do not fear forgiving."[1]

Power Passage

Be kind and compassionate to one another, forgiving each other, just as Christ God forgave you. Be imitators of God, therefore, as dearly loved children and live a life of love, just as Christ loved us and gave himself up for us as a fragrant offering and sacrifice to God. (Ephesians 4:32–5:2 NIV)

Point of Practice

I've had the pleasure of having tea in the home of the honorable Nelson Mandela. To look at the face of the jovial, wise man, you would never imagine that he endured the horrors of apartheid. He is a gracious man of strength, always encouraging others. He is always thinking of his fellow South Africans. Despite everything he has been through, he continues to fight for the rights of underserved and underprivileged people. He went from a prisoner to the presidency. I love the part of his speech that says, "If we hate them then they win. God has given us the ability to forgive!"

Most of us can barely fathom the isolation and pain that Mandela suffered. We can only imagine the kind of hurt that stems from such heartache and what it takes to overcome it.

When people have wronged me, my natural instinct is to hold it inside, get upset, and feel hurt. But every injustice, small or big, deserves mercy. God calls us to be gracious imitators of His grace, people with big enough character and heart to walk hand in hand with those who hurt us.

Sometimes we stumble and must rely on Him to pick us up. If we are to hope for grace in our own misgivings, we must be willing to extend it to those who deserve it.

Nelson Mandela shows us that the greatest pain can be met with grace. God has equipped us with the strength to build bridges of forgiveness, and it's in our hands to choose to walk across them.

Point of Prayer

God, thank You for the gift of forgiveness. I am aware of Your mercy and love in my life, and I claim the presence of Your grace and wisdom today and always. I open my heart to the power of Your endless love and know that because I forgive, I am forgiven.

10 Pensive Points

To forgive those who have hurt us in some way is not always easy, but it is the Lord's greatest gift to us. Consider spending some time writing down a few hurts, recent or long past, and then read through the following points. Alexander Pope said, "To err is human, to forgive divine." Do you forgive your way or God's way?

1. What is one quality you possess similar to the qualities you've just read about in Nelson Mandela's story?

2. What most inspires you about the way Mandela is a gracious imitator of God?

3. What is the most recent instance of your forgiving another person in your life?

4. Do you consider anything "unforgivable"? Do you hold grudges easily?

5. What pains from the past are still fresh in your memory? What makes those pains so fresh in your memory? Are you gaining anything from carrying around the memory? What makes grudges worthwhile?

6. Who are you upset with right now? Name five reasons why you haven't already resolved the conflict.

7. According to Ephesians 4:32–5:2, how is God instructing you to respond to this situation?

8. Think of sins you've committed in the past. How have your friends responded to the pain you've inflicted? How did you want them to treat you?

9. What one thing is stopping you from treating others the way you want to be treated?

10. Think of one small way you can become a gracious imitator of God today.

Power Passage

Why do you look at the speck of sawdust in your brother's eye and pay no attention to the plank in your own eye? How can you say to your brother, "Let me take the speck out of your eye," when all the time there is a plank in your own eye? You hypocrite, first take the plank out of your own eye, and then you will see clearly to remove the speck from your brother's eye. (Matthew 7:3–5 NIV)

Forgiveness Extends from Heaven to Earth

God gives me the strength to forgive.

Forgiveness is a huge word that carries a lot of weight in the kingdom. Your blessings are tied to forgiveness. Your miracles are tied to forgiveness. Even your answered prayers are tied to forgiveness.

We've already discussed that forgiveness is really for you, not the person you are forgiving. Why? Because God knows that you cannot truly love without forgiveness. Many people move from one relationship to another, hurting innocent people along the way because of their unwillingness to forgive. Perhaps someone has hurt them, so the second something goes wrong between them and their friend, significant other, boss, or some other person they are in relationship with, instead of expressing their feelings, instead of admitting that they are hurt, they shut down, they cut off the person and vow that the next relationship will be different. They promise themselves they will never allow anyone to get close enough to hurt them again.

I can speak of these things only because I learned early in my life to be quick to forgive. I've learned that when I look to the Lord in my times of deepest hurt, He will always open wide the doors of mercy. In my grief, He will show me that I must make room for the power of grace for others, as I need the power of grace myself.

I was married for the first time when I was in my early twenties. I knew before the wedding that going through with the marriage was a mistake. I knew I wasn't supposed to marry him. Still, rather than listening to and following God's lead, I allowed myself to be led by my pride. The invitations were sent, all kinds of money had been spent, and I didn't want to call things off and be embarrassed. It was a mistake. Eventually, after feeling emotionally neglected, I saw the marriage end in divorce.

I am, however, thankful for the experience. I learned some very valuable lessons about myself and about life from that situation, and I also learned about the power of forgiveness. I had to forgive myself for ignoring my instincts—God's voice. I had to forgive my ex-husband for the hurtful things he did and said. I emerged from that experience smarter and stronger and steadfast in my belief that God never leaves us. I also learned that moving on in life is directly tied to our willingness to forgive others and ourselves.

Learn to forgive so that you can live a life of joy and experience all the blessings God wants to offer you every single day.

Remember the story of Joseph and his coat of many colors. He knew all about the power of forgiveness.

The Favored Son

Jacob was a man with two wives, two concubines, twelve sons, and one daughter. While numerous issues are recorded about Jacob's family, most problems centered on Joseph—Jacob's eleventh son, but the firstborn of his wife Rachel.

Joseph was, without a doubt, his father's favorite. He was young and bold, and his father continually lavished him with praise and gifts, in particular a beautiful coat. On top of blessings from his earthly father, Joseph had been given the uncommon ability to interpret dreams. At a young seventeen years old, he received a vision of the Lord's big plans for his life. He shared the promises with his family, but they didn't respond kindly. His brothers, jealous and angry, called him "the dreamer" and plotted a way to get rid of him.

Out in the field one day, Joseph's brothers saw an opportunity to do away with him. They stripped him of his coat and threw him in a hole, discussing together the best way to murder their brother in secret. As they talked over their meal, a group of merchants came by. The brothers realized by murdering Joseph they would gain nothing; it would be more profitable and equally as effective to sell him. They stopped the merchants and handed over Joseph for a mere twenty pieces of silver. As an alibi, his brothers kept his coat, dousing it in goat's blood, and took it back to their father to prove that Joseph was dead.

The favorite son was now at the mercy of his masters. As the years progressed, Joseph was led through numerous trials. He was sold into slavery in Egypt and became a servant for one of Pharaoh's officials, Potiphar. Quickly earning the favor of Potiphar, he again encountered trouble when Potiphar's wife tried to seduce him. He wouldn't consent. Hurt by his refusal, she lied about Joseph to Potiphar, who threw his most loyal servant into prison. But Joseph trusted in the promise he had received in his youth, even in the darkest hours of being betrayed and imprisoned.

In prison Joseph received God's grace. Behind bars he met Pharaoh's cupbearer and interpreted his dreams. In return he asked the cupbearer to remember him when he was restored to power. Two years after this incident, Pharaoh began to have dreams. He was greatly troubled by the images in his sleep and the cupbearer told him about Joseph's vision. Pharaoh immediately called Joseph up from the cells and listened intently as Joseph told him of the imminent famine.

Sensing God's presence and Joseph's great wisdom, Pharaoh said, "Since God has made all this known to you, there is no one so discerning and wise as you. You shall be in charge of my palace, and all my people are to submit to your orders. Only with respect to the throne will I be greater than you" (Genesis 41:39–40 NIV).

So the boy who came to Egypt as a slave became the second-most powerful person in Egypt, fulfilling the dreams of his youth that God would install him in a position of power.

When the famine Joseph had foreseen in Pharaoh's dream approached, Joseph's father sent his remaining sons to Egypt to bring back food for the family. While they didn't know it yet, the very brothers who sold Joseph into slavery were to come face-to-face with the one they betrayed, and they would have to ask for his help and kindness.

When Joseph saw his brothers, he had every right to be angry with them. They had sold him into slavery and lied about his death, abandoned him to a life of misery. But instead of feeling great anger and resentment, Joseph saw the good that had come from their actions. He was forgiving.

When he revealed himself to his family, he compassionately reassured them, "Don't be afraid. Am I in the place of God?" (Genesis 50:19 NIV). "You intended to harm me, but God intended it for good to accomplish what is now being done, the saving of many lives. So then, don't be afraid. I will provide for you and your children" (50:20–21 NIV).

Power Passage

If you forgive men when they sin against you, your heavenly Father will also forgive you. (Matthew 6:14 NIV)

Point of Practice

The great lesson of Joseph and his brothers is forgiveness. Joseph met life's most difficult circumstances as the result of his brothers' hatred, but he was able to persevere through the hurt. Instead of choosing animosity, he chose love.

Often in life when we're wronged, we allow bitterness and hate to accumulate. Forgiveness seems too difficult. While in the short run we might enjoy revenge, in the long run we hurt only ourselves.

Consider a hurt you're holding on to. What is it bringing you? Is it worthwhile? A lack of forgiveness is only giving you a lack of love. Read the story of Joseph again in Genesis chapters 37–50 and ask God for the ability to bestow genuine brotherly forgiveness. Opportunities are plentiful for those who can set down their baggage of hate and move forward.

Point of Prayer

God, I claim the freedom Your forgiveness offers me in life. I open myself to the joy and peace Your grace and forgiveness provide me. I walk through life lightly, free of resentment and bathed in Your love.

10 Pensive Points

Think about the members of your family or your close friends and the status of your relationships with them. Perhaps go through some old photos or a box of mementos to remind you who is important to you. Are there people you've had disagreements with? People you no longer speak to? Think about the times you needed to forgive some of them and the times you needed to be forgiven.

1. What about the story of Joseph most affects you?

2. Think of one way your family dynamic is similar to that of Joseph and his brothers.

3. Recall one time when you were jealous. How did you cope with that emotion?

4. Joseph has an incredible sense of faith and belief in the Lord. How does your faith allow you to forgive in your difficult moments?

5. God calls us not to forget, but to forgive. Think back on a situation where you have been able to react compassionately.

6. Were you able to remove the hurt to see the hand of God in that situation?

7. What is the greatest act of forgiveness you've witnessed in your life?

8. What is one thing that makes it especially hard to forgive family?

9. Make a list of whom you have had to forgive and who has had to forgive you. How has forgiveness helped your relationships?

10. Write on your calendar one small way you can show brotherly forgiveness today.

Power Passage

When you stand praying, if you hold anything against anyone, forgive him, so that your Father in heaven may forgive you your sins. (Mark 11:25 NIV)

Nothing I Have Done Is Beyond the Forgiveness of God

I receive unlimited mercy.

How do we deal with matters so complicated they seem unfathomable, situations we can't even talk about? As children of God, we've learned to believe in an amazing concept: unlimited mercy. Nothing we have done or will ever do is beyond His infinite understanding and grace—nothing. Think about that. It's a pretty awesome statement to make: There is nothing a believer can do to separate himself or herself from God's mercy.

A recent television show about the power of forgiveness illustrated this very concept. As I watched, I wondered: If the same thing happened to me, could I find a way to forgive?

One New Year's Eve Katy Hutchison and her husband, Bob McIntosh, were having a quiet dinner with friends. After dinner Bob went over to a vacationing neighbor's house to check on things because he had heard their son was having an unsupervised party. He arrived to find more than two hundred out-of-control teenagers using alcohol and drugs in the house. He tried to break up the festivities and was punched by one of the partygoers, then knocked down and kicked in the head. He died of a massive brain hemorrhage.

No one came forward with any information about who had murdered Bob. It was five years later when Ryan Aldridge was finally convicted and sent to jail for the crime. He served three out of the five years he received for his manslaughter conviction and was then released on parole. Today, as unbelievable as it may seem, Ryan and Katy Hutchison travel together giving talks to young people in schools about the dangers of unsupervised partying and alcohol and drug use. The two are living examples of the power of forgiveness.

This story is such a strong example of the depths to which forgiveness can change our lives if we choose to embrace it. Forgiveness didn't just change Katy's life, it changed Ryan's too. Rather than hate, Katy made the choice to look for a lesson in what happened to Bob. Her heartbreak aside, Katy knew she could not live in unforgiveness and hate; she and her children had already lost so much. It is hard to imagine a scenario where forgiveness would be more difficult. Still, like Jesus on the cross, Katy found it in her heart, despite her incredible pain, to forgive the very person who stole the life of her husband and killed her children's father.

Katy exemplifies the ways God's gift of grace and forgiveness can heal even the most broken heart, and as the recipient of that forgiveness, Ryan represents proof that God's mercy is for everyone, not just those people whom we find easy to love.[1]

I know another amazing story of forgiveness. Dick Fiske was just nineteen years old when the planes came to bomb Pearl Harbor. He had enlisted in the U.S. Marine Corps in February 1940 at the age of seventeen. By July of that year, he was stationed in Pearl Harbor. He made his home on the USS *West Virginia* as a bugler without any idea of what would come his way.

On a bright sunny morning, December 7, 1941, he was standing on the deck of the battleship when Japanese fighter planes launched a surprise attack and declared war on the United States. Roughly 2,400 lives were taken by 350 Japanese fighters. The U.S. Pacific Fleet was largely demolished. One of the greatest fighting forces in the world was left stunned.

Like so many others at Pearl Harbor, Dick Fiske was angry: "I hated so much. The hate that I had put me in the hospital for three and a half months with bleeding ulcers. I almost died." At the time, he couldn't think of the faces behind enemy lines, who they were and where they came from. All he could see was the hurt they had created.

On the other side of the battle that morning was Zenji Abe, a Japanese dive-bomber in his mid-twenties. On December 7, his plane flew over Pearl Harbor at nine in the morning, sending the second shock wave of bombs onto the Pacific Fleet. The bombs he dropped took the lives of many of the friends and shipmates Dick mourned. When he was in battle, he wasn't thinking of the sons he was killing or the fathers he was taking away; like the U.S. soldiers at Pearl Harbor, he was doing his job.

Abe and Fiske both survived World War II, emerging with reverence for their countries and those who chose to serve. Fiske continued his work in the military, serving in the Korean and Vietnam wars. After retiring in the seventies, he started volunteering at Pearl Harbor's Arizona Memorial. While his anger had peaked immediately following the war, the pursuant years had taught him the tradition of service. He learned to believe that each country's people had moved forward in pursuit of what they thought was right. The fighters in Japan who had dropped the bombs and sent the torpedoes were serving just as he had. Fiske began his work reaching out to veterans, trying to build a bridge of understanding between the two sides.

In the 1980s, Abe too began his stride toward reconciliation and finding peace. He made his first trip back to Pearl Harbor since 1941. In the company of ten other Japanese pilots, he visited the Arizona Memorial. They had no idea how they would be received, if at all. There were some, certainly, who wouldn't want to shake his hand, but he would welcome those who did.

The park rangers welcomed Abe and the other contrite pilots. For them too it was a time for healing.

In 1991, fifty years after Pearl Harbor, a World War II reunion took place, bringing together fighters from both sides. It was there that Fiske met Abe, and an unlikely but precious friendship emerged.

After finding common ground on the land that once placed them on separate sides, Fiske and Abe began a commemorative ritual. Annually, Abe would send Fiske five hundred dollars to buy flowers to place at the Arizona Memorial, a tribute of his sadness for the hurt he had caused and his promise for a peaceful future. In turn, Fiske would take the flowers and play taps for those whose lives had been lost. It was a gesture of reconciliation and peace between two enemies who had learned to become friends.[2]

Power Passage

You are a forgiving God, gracious and compassionate, slow to anger and abounding in love. Therefore you did not desert them. (Nehemiah 9:17 NIV)

Point of Practice

First Peter 1:3–4 says, "Praise be to the God and Father of our Lord Jesus Christ! In his great mercy he has given us new birth into a living hope through the resurrection of Jesus Christ from the dead, and into an inheritance that can never perish, spoil or fade" (NIV).

Unlimited mercy gives us a new lease on life. We have hope for a future that isn't burdened by our sins of the past. God asks us to render unlimited mercy toward others. By extending forgiveness to those who wrong us, we will be able to give new life to troubled relationships.

We all know people we should have forgiven long ago. Do it right now! Forgive right now! You probably should start with yourself! Forgive yourself for choices you made long ago. Okay, you've made some mistakes; we all have. Guess what? We'll make even more. Forgive the person or people who hurt you now! They don't know and probably don't care that you're hurting. I care! That's why I'm urging you now to pray this prayer with me. Hey, it worked for me; it will work for you.

Point of Prayer

Dear God, I am hurting and I need Your help. _____ hurt me, and I have tried on my own to forget. I know You have the power and presence to help me forgive. Forgiving is an act of faith. And since faith pleases You, I forgive _____. I will not rehearse my hurt and pain. I let go of the past and move forward by faith. My heart is open now to the love and joy You will fill it with. I will not remind _____ of the pain he or she caused me. I do this so You can forgive me of my wrong. I know this will be a day-by-day process, so I yield my will and my emotions to You. And in the name of Jesus, I declare victory over unforgiveness.

10 Pensive Points

Sometimes it can be difficult to offer forgiveness; in fact, it can be very hard work. When we remember how we have been forgiven, though, we can find it easier to forgive others. Reflect on situations where someone has offered you forgiveness. Think about your parents or a special friend who always accepts you unconditionally and forgives you no matter what. What kind of work do you need to do to forgive all those who have hurt you?

1. What might Abe and Fiske have had to do to prepare themselves to find common ground and be open to friendship after such extensive pain?

2. Whom have you forgiven?

3. Think about the lives of the soldiers who reconciled versus those who held on to their pain. Who do you think is better off and why?

4. Whom have you been unable to forgive?

5. Whom have you shown unlimited mercy to?

6. Who has shown unlimited mercy to you?

7. How has that person's extravagant displays of grace had an impact on your life?

8. Reflect on your relationship with Christ. Do you believe He has extended unlimited mercy to you? Do you believe He holds anything against you?

9. List three ways your life is more plentiful because of forgiveness.

10. Set a forgiveness goal for today.

Power Passage

In him we have redemption through his blood, the forgiveness of sins, in accordance with the riches of God's grace that he lavished on us with all wisdom and understanding. (Ephesians 1:7–8 NIV)

Inner Honesty Births
Outward Grace

Each day I have the opportunity to begin anew in God.

One of the most healing and liberating gifts of the Lord is His forgiveness. He freely and openly extends His mercy, which has the power to drastically change our lives. We have to admit we need mercy in order to experience its beauty. It's easy to see the struggles of others but be deluded about our own.

"I'm Gonna Be Ready," one of the songs from my album *Believe*, captures the essence and effect of God's forgiveness in our lives. God can renew our lives with grace if we place our trust in Him. Treating God's gift of forgiveness with reverence and respect, sharing it with others as the Lord has shared it with us, is our task as Christians. Learning to be honest about our own weaknesses and sins enables us to give up our heaviest burdens to the Lord and move forward in the richness of the Holy Spirit's grace. God's forgiveness is ours and waiting to be claimed whenever we need it, no matter what or who we think we are.

Every society has those who are considered "less than" others: people with undesirable jobs, people who make money through means that seem unfair or corrupt. In biblical days, tax collectors were such people.

During Jesus' time, tax collectors were considered the pit bulls of the government. Tax collectors collaborated with the undesirable Roman authorities. They worked locally, forcing their own people to pay government debts. Beyond this, however, tax collectors were given authority to charge however much they wanted. They pocketed any excess they were able to make off individuals. Numerous tax collectors took advantage of their authority and forced individuals to pay more than they could bear. Tax collectors became dreaded figures and symbols of greed and corruption.

According to Luke 19, Zacchaeus was a wealthy tax collector. As a result of his greed and selfishness, Zacchaeus spent his life largely alone, outcast from those over whom he exerted his power.

But when Jesus came to the city, Zacchaeus was curious to see the man people were talking about with such excitement. However, he was very short in stature, and he knew no one would go out of his or her way to help him see Jesus when He came. Determined to see the Lord for himself, he resorted to climbing a sycamore tree, watching the road from a high perch.

When Jesus walked down the street, He didn't pass as Zacchaeus expected but instead stopped and told him to climb down from the tree. Jesus said He wanted to spend the day with the man with whom no one else wanted to associate.

The crowd was shocked. They could hardly believe a man so renowned for being good would stoop so low as to visit the house of a sinner. But Jesus didn't listen to the rumblings of others. He knew He had come for the lost and broken. He knew He had come for everyone, even people like Zacchaeus.

With the Lord in his house, Zacchaeus had a change of heart. He acted immediately to apologize to those he'd wronged and to make restitution to those he'd robbed. He saw the grace of the Lord and realized he desperately needed it in his own life. Zacchaeus stood up and said to the Lord, "Look, Lord! Here and now I give half of my possessions to the poor, and if I have cheated anybody out of anything, I will pay back four times the amount" (Luke 19:8 NIV).

Jesus responded to Zacchaeus the same way He responds to all of those who are willing to lay down their sins to walk in the truth. He declared, "Today salvation has come to this house, because this man, too, is a son of Abraham. For the Son of Man came to seek and to save what was lost" (Luke 19:9–10 NIV).

Power Passage

All the prophets testify about him that everyone who believes in him receives forgiveness of sins through his name. (Acts 10:43 NIV)

Point of Practice

It's hard for us to imagine what it would have been like seeing Jesus acknowledge Zacchaeus in a crowd, singling him out above all others to be His companion and friend. Everyone was likely appalled at the mere image of the miracle worker in the company of such an immoral person. It would have been equivalent to Jesus' breaking bread with drug dealers and criminals, hustlers and prostitutes today.

But God has always shared His table with such people. He has constantly shown us that mercy exists even for the destitute and deplorable. All can be redeemed. The story of Zacchaeus shows us mercy on two levels. First, it demonstrates the call to open up our lives to those who most need friendship and caring. It's easy to go through our daily existence in our box of comfort, spending our time with those we know best and who are most like us. But as Jesus showed us, there's a world outside our own lives full of individuals who need love and mercy. While it might be contrary to our instincts, we should welcome opportunities to expand the kinds of people we let into our world, closing the door to none and showing mercy to all.

Second, Zacchaeus's story shows us that no one is beyond redemption. He was one of the most despised individuals in Jericho. His corruption was his most dominant trait. But when Jesus saw Zacchaeus, He didn't see his sins; He saw his potential. God offers us the same clean canvas. No matter what we've done or how we've acted, He sees what we can be and welcomes us to pursue God's plan for us. If we're willing to claim grace and bestow it generously on others, the rewards in our lives now and our lives to come will be plentiful.

Point of Prayer

God, what a blessing to know that no matter what I have done, I am worthy of Your grace. This is a great responsibility and I take this gift very seriously. I am renewed in Your love and know that You forgive me before I even make the request.

10 Pensive Points

As Christians we are tasked with giving the gift of forgiveness to others as God has given it to us. That doesn't just include the people it's easy to forgive, but it also includes those who we may not think, because of our biases and prejudices, deserve it. God says that everyone deserves it. Are there any Zacchaeuses in your life?

1. Is your initial reaction to the story of Zacchaeus, who had harmed people and lived a corrupt life, that he should have received the Lord's grace?

2. Whom do you consider outcasts? At whose house would you least expect to see Jesus?

3. Whom have you met that you're unwilling to share a table with?

4. What inhibits you from opening your arms to the kingdom's most needy and broken?

5. Name one way in which you are like Zacchaeus.

6. Write in your journal what it means to you to "claim grace."

7. Compose your own prayer to seek the grace of God.

8. Meeting Jesus transformed Zacchaeus, and he thereafter lived a life of repentance. What one change have you made as a result of knowing Jesus and realizing your sins?

9. Write on your calendar for today one specific thing you can start to do to more genuinely live in the Lord's grace.

10. Create a definition of *grace* in your own words.

Power Passage

If we claim to be without sin, we deceive ourselves and the truth is not in us. If we confess our sins, he is faithful and just and will forgive us our sins and purify us from all unrighteousness. (1 John 1:8–9 NIV)

Chapter Four

THE POWER OF CONFESSION

"Forgetting what is behind and straining toward what is ahead, I press on toward the goal to win the prize for which God has called me heavenward in Christ Jesus."

—*Philippians 3:13–14* NIV

Confession Is Acknowledging the Grace of God

All I have to do is ask the Savior for help.

God's grace is always with us. To activate it, all we need to do is call on it. We often wait to reach out to God for only the bigger things, but the truth is God is also there for us in our daily challenges, in those issues that pop up again and again, for those habits that we keep trying to let go of but for some reason just can't. For some of us it's lust, for others greed, for some it's lying, and for others it's substance abuse. While our individual sins might be different, the struggle is the same: something we just can't seem to beat.

My song "It's Time to Change" is about this very issue—those things in our lives that we keep doing, knowing full well those habits aren't pleasing in God's eyes. My challenge was people pleasing. For years I tried to turn my "yeses" into "nos." It wasn't that I didn't want to help my friends, family, and others when they needed me. I am the oldest of six children, so I spent a good amount of time helping care for my younger siblings. Long before my daughter was born I had a mothering kind of personality.

I always thought of my family before I thought of myself. And I bring that persona to the work I do, to my ministry. When you are a minister you have to work and cooperate with people. The central theme of ministry is helping others, and I believe I was put on this earth to do just that.

The problem was I started to feel like I was spread too thin. I was losing myself. I wanted so much to help everyone who needed it, but the result was that my own priorities suffered. I tried everything—saying no, being strong, keeping lists and calendars—but nothing worked. The song is centered on one of the most powerful truths about God. The Lord is a persistent Father who will never leave us or forsake us. We only need to stop putting off until tomorrow what we need to change today.

If there is some habit or pattern in your life you wish to let go of, turn it over to God. The Holy Spirit has shown me that no matter how many times the Lord has to travel to the same doorstep to pick up our broken bodies, He will come each time with arms outstretched, and like the father in the parable of the prodigal son, saying what we always need to hear: *Welcome home.*

Let's take a look at that parable. A man had two sons. As in many families today, the man's two sons were very different. The older was steadfast and responsible; the younger had a penchant for adventure. The elder son stayed home and worked the family's land. The younger son wanted to see the world and what he could make of it.

The younger son asked his father for his share of the inheritance. While it wasn't the customary procedure, his father agreed and divvied up his estate accordingly. With money in hand, the young son went out and lived what he thought was a full life, indulging all his desires. He quickly squandered his inheritance and found himself penniless and in desperate need of help. He was ashamed of his ways and what his family might say, so instead of returning home, he looked for work. He got a job feeding pigs, a job so lowly the animals ate better than he did.

As a famine hit the country and his circumstances became worse and worse, he knew, despite his embarrassment, he would have to return home. But his head hung low with his poor decisions. He thought he had been too irresponsible to return home as a son. Instead, he would beg his father to be merciful and hire him to work. He played the dialogue over and over again in his head: "Father, I have sinned against heaven and against you. I am no longer worthy to be called your son; make me like one of your hired men" (Luke 15:18–19 NIV). With a small degree of hope, he headed toward home and prayed for mercy.

The return did not go at all as he had planned. His father saw him from a long way off and came running; he greeted his son compassionately with kisses and hugs. While the son offered his rehearsed plea, his father disregarded it. "Quick!" he said to his servants. "Bring the best robe and put it on him. Put a ring on his finger and sandals on his feet. Bring the fattened calf and kill it. Let's have a feast and celebrate. For this son of mine was dead and is alive again; he was lost and is found" (15:22–24 NIV).

While a celebration commenced, the older brother returned from another hard day's work. He saw the great joy surrounding his brother's return, but instead of feeling relief, he felt envy. His father came out from the party and begged the older brother to come in, but he refused. He was deeply hurt. For many years, he'd been responsible. He had worked diligently and obediently. He had given all he had to his father and hadn't received so much as a small party in return. His younger brother, however, could go out, squander everything, live immorally, and still return to a feast of magnificent grandeur.

The father felt compassion, but he said, "My son, you are always with me, and everything I have is yours. But we had to celebrate and be glad, because this brother of yours was dead and is alive again; he was lost and is found" (Luke 15:31–32 NIV).

Power Passage

Answer me when I call to you,
>   O my righteous God.
Give me relief from my distress;
>   be merciful to me and hear my prayer.
(Psalm 4:1 NIV)

Point of Practice

For many, the parable of the prodigal son is one of the most difficult lessons to embrace in the Bible. In our society, we measure success and reward against the effort we're willing to give. Grace and celebration for the reckless are inappropriate. We want justice and fairness more than forgiveness. We want what is right more than what is kind.

This parable is full of treasures we can apply daily. If we are to be like Jesus, we have to focus on the rewards of confession. When we confess, God readily forgives. Never hold in sin, guilt, or feelings of inadequacies, for God is our ever-present help!

While we might not like to believe it, we've all been, in some way, the prodigal son. We have squandered parts of our lives carelessly, leaving the glory promised to us for the bigger glory we believe we can find elsewhere. For years some get wrapped up in their work. Some get lost in sexual immorality. Some develop profane mouths, and some have self-driven motives.

Like the prodigal son, when we realize the neglect of our actions and the lack of fulfillment that comes from our careless ways, we too return to the Father, embarrassed, with our faces downcast.

And while we expect to go back begging for grace and mercy, the Lord runs to us with open arms and throws a massive celebration. He isn't as concerned with where we went or how we behaved. He's simply overjoyed that we have finally made our way back to Him, that our own curvy roads have led us home, confessing our mistakes.

God has taught me that not a day will pass where He closes the gates to say, "This time you have gone too far. I've had enough." His forgiveness is limitless, His arms always outstretched. God is waiting patiently and eagerly for all us prodigals to come home, confessing our sins.

Point of Prayer

God, I turn over my struggles to You. I open myself to You, Holy Spirit, and invite You in to help me release all habits that are not pleasing to You. I ask for Your healing deep in my soul so I may be all You created me to be.

10 Pensive Points

Do you have habits, patterns, or addictions that keep you from living the life you want? Are there things in your life that you want or need to let go of? We can turn to God at any time and share those things we struggle with. How would your life be different if you shared your struggles with God?

1. In the parable of the prodigal son, do you identify more with the older son or the younger son?

2. Was the father's reaction to the son's return fair? If so, what made it fair?

3. Can you understand the older son's reaction? Think of a situation in which you responded in the same way.

4. Think about how we all are prodigal sons in relation to God.

5. Is there something you've been struggling with that you could turn over to God for help?

6. List ways you have seen God's persistent forgiveness in action.

7. What is one instance where you wandered knowingly from the truth? How did it feel to return?

8. Do you believe God's door is always open to you, no matter what?

9. Knowing the unlimited nature of God's forgiveness, how will you treat fellow sons returning home?

10. How can you learn to step into the banquet of God's celebration?

Power Passage

I waited patiently for the LORD;
>   he turned to me and heard my cry.
He lifted me out of the slimy pit,
>   out of the mud and mire;
he set my feet on a rock
>   and gave me a firm place to stand.
He put a new song in my mouth,
>   a hymn of praise to our God.
Many will see and fear
>   and put their trust in the LORD.
>   (Psalm 40:1–3 NIV)

I Need Mercy;
I Am Wounded

God grants me grace abundantly.

God is a merciful God. His mercy is so incredible, so big and unwavering, it is hard for us as humans to conceive. There is nothing in this earthly world that we can compare it to. And all we need to do to access it is to simply call on it, ask for it.

Still, sometimes we find ourselves in a place spiritually where we just don't feel we deserve God's love and mercy. We might know in our hearts that God always forgives us, but in our heads we think this time we've done something too terrible to even approach God to ask for the Holy Spirit's grace.

If you ever feel this way, you are not alone. No matter how long we've trusted and believed in God, all of us still have times where we believe there is no forgiveness for some things. The good news is, even if we think it, it is not true. There is nothing God won't forgive us for. God never chooses us based on our pasts. If that were the case, none of us would qualify for forgiveness or mercy. Even when we think we don't deserve it, He forgives, again and again. That's the essence of God, and we should never forget it.

Never let your mistakes condemn you! Every time you hear that negative voice speak, forcefully rebuke it by saying: "There is now no condemnation for those who are in Christ Jesus" (Romans 8:1 NIV).

Let's look at how Jesus illustrated this truth. On one of the many occasions when He accepted an invitation, Jesus was the dinner guest of a religious leader, a Pharisee named Simon. As was common, word of Jesus' arrival swept through the city. A woman in town who was burdened greatly with the sins in her life heard the news. She desperately needed the comforting words of a healer and went to the Pharisee's house looking for Jesus.

While the Pharisee was busy, the woman came and sat at Jesus' feet. Overcome, she began weeping. Her tears of regret and pain fell on Him; she wiped Jesus' feet with her hair and poured her bottle of perfume on Jesus' feet.

As the woman was doing this, Simon returned. Instead of seeing a humble woman in need, he saw a sinner. "If this man were a prophet," he said, "he would know who is touching him and what kind of woman she is—that she is a sinner" (Luke 7:39 NIV).

Instead of responding in embarrassment for being associated with such a woman, Jesus responded in kindness:

Do you see this woman? I came into your house. You did not give me any water for my feet, but she wet my feet with her tears and wiped them with her hair. You did not give me a kiss, but this woman, from the time I entered, has not stopped kissing my feet. You did not put oil on my head, but she has poured perfume on my feet. Therefore, I tell you, her many sins have been forgiven—for she loved much. But he who has been forgiven little loves little. (Luke 7:44–47 NIV)

Power Passage

He took up our infirmities and carried our diseases. (Matthew 8:17 NIV)

Point of Practice

I love how the Word of God is so practical even in today's society. Simon misinterpreted the actions of this woman. She gave true and pure worship with love and respect to Jesus by anointing Him with her valuable perfume. These actions were her admission that she was wounded. They were her confession. What God expects of us is our admission that we need His mercy and His unfailing, unconditional love.

If we confess our sins, God is faithful and just to forgive us. It doesn't matter what people say—God's opinion and love for us are all that matters! Just make sure you don't remain in the sin that separates you from God. Confess, admit you're wounded. God forgives even when man doesn't.

Point of Prayer

God, I humbly request Your mercy for my sin of _____. I move ahead in my life today knowing that I am blessed by Your forgiveness. I proceed in my life with the intention of treating others as You have treated me, with patience, kindness, understanding, and grace.

10 Pensive Points

God's forgiveness is not only for us, but it is for all those who believe in the Lord. You know you can bring any sin to God in confession. Do you allow others to do the same? Do you believe in fairness or forgiveness?

1. How were Simon the Pharisee and the sinful woman similar? How were they different? Did their differences matter to Jesus?

2. What did the sinful woman understand that Simon did not?

3. Go back and read Luke 7:41–43. What does this parable say about the lesson Jesus is teaching Simon?

4. Simon relies heavily on appearance and ritual. As long as things look "right" and are done "right," he's okay. In what ways are you like Simon? How does what looks right have an impact on your faith in the Lord?

5. Who might view you as being like Simon? What obstructs them from seeing your need of God's grace?

6. List three ways you think you are in need of more grace than others.

7. List three people you think are in need of more grace than you.

8. Remember a time it was difficult for you to admit when you faltered.

9. How did you feel once you admitted it?

10. Write on your calendar a specific request for mercy that you will bring to the Lord today.

Power Passage

Jesus said, "It is not the healthy who need a doctor, but the sick. But go and learn what this means: 'I desire mercy, not sacrifice.' For I have not come to call the righteous, but sinners." (Matthew 9:12–13 NIV)

Confession Makes Room for Happiness

It opens the door to joy.

I've heard it a million times. So have you. Our mothers, teachers, friends, and mentors have told us: "We are our own worst critics." But it doesn't have to be that way. Through God's inevitable grace, we are able to move forward to a place of healing and hope. By opening the door to honesty, we also open the door to joy.

That's why I love music so much, especially gospel music. It is a powerful force that touches upon the wide range of emotions we deal with in the spectrum of life. Many people think of gospel music as something to help us through our trials, which it does, but gospel music is also about giving God praise; it's about celebrating life; it's about hope and joy.

One of the easiest and fastest ways to get in touch with the good in life is to show God gratitude. Sometimes when I am having a bad day I catch myself and say, "Yolanda, count your blessings." I stop for a minute and think about all the good in my life: my family that loves me, my wonderful friends and colleagues, the success I've had in my career, and of course the love of my life, my little daughter. And those are just a few examples! Sometimes I get started counting my blessings and I can't stop.

What is more joyful than spending some time thinking about all the gifts God has given you? That's the message in my song "Believe." No matter what happened in your life ten or twenty years ago, no matter what is happening today, never, ever give up. You can't see your blessings if you are focused on all that is wrong in your life, on your past and on the mistakes you've made. Confess your sins to God, let go of the past, focus on what is good in your life, and keep on working toward your goals. God is good all the time. No matter what you've done, what mistakes you've made, proceed through life with a grateful, hopeful heart, and the Lord will reward you with immeasurable goodness and love.

The story of William Wilson is an example of exactly what can happen when we bring God into our struggles. William knew what it was to battle with the bottle. He was ten when his father left. That man had drunk himself out of Vermont straight up to Canada. His mother left soon after, choosing a career in medicine over a career in parenting. Wilson spent the remainder of his young years under the care of his grandparents.

By the time he was twenty-two, Wilson had forgotten about the effects of drinking. He had forgotten how alcohol abuse could tear families apart, and how his father's alcoholism had left him lonely. He was a man in the army, a young officer, and he found no harm in a beer among good friends. At first his intake was harmless. Then one drink turned to many and beer turned to liquor. A few cocktails in, he felt the pleasure of honest lips; it was a liquid switch that pried him loose from uncomfortable banter and quiet friends.

"Even that first evening I got thoroughly drunk," he wrote, "and within the next time or two I passed out completely. But as everyone drank hard, not too much was made of that." One excuse birthed another, and Wilson was quickly on his way to alcoholism.

After his stint in the army, the years ticked off. He was married in 1918, just before World War I. Wilson's addiction to drink was solidified. When he got back from the war, he moved to New York and headed to Wall Street. His success was mixed with sadness, and he turned to the bottle to deal with his bouts of heartache and celebrate his moments of triumph. The bottle became his business.

With his ever-worsening dependence on drink and the crash of the economy, Wilson's business relationships fell to pieces, and he couldn't keep a job. By the time he was thirty-eight, he had gone from being a successful businessman on Wall Street to being virtually unemployable.

His wife's family generously took them in. It looked as though the once-promising Wilson had followed the route of his father, a man devastated by drink. He became prone to bar fights and blackouts. He was admitted to the Charles B. Towns Hospital for Drug and Alcohol Addictions four times and was told his problems were medical, not moral. He could not overcome it, they said. His choices were two: he would die from the drink or be locked up.

One of his old drinking buddies, Ebby Thatcher, had come clean with the Oxford Group Movement—a Protestant group that embraced the promises of divine guidance and confession to get sober. Thatcher visited Wilson after one of Wilson's stints in the hospital. Wilson tested it out. He was skeptical; he had been an atheist since his youth. He could hardly find Thatcher's conversion believable. "Last summer an alcoholic crackpot," Wilson said of Thatcher. "Now, I suspected, a little cracked about religion."

But despite his skepticism, the words of encouragement, spirituality, and hope got his brain turning. During his last stint in the Charles B. Towns Hospital, he yelled at God to show Himself, hardly believing such an occurrence was possible. But then, as Wilson wrote later, "suddenly my room blazed with an indescribably white light. I was seized with an ecstasy beyond description. Every joy I had known was pale by comparison." It was his miracle moment that simultaneously birthed religious conviction and sobriety.

Wilson held on to his sobriety as much as he could. He was careful and guarded, but as life's difficulties mounted, he desired the comforting shoulder of the familiar bottle. Wilson realized that the best way to stay sober was with the support of others who were struggling. No one could do it alone.

In his desperate desire for a drink and his need of a friend, he reached out to a stranger. He contacted Dr. Robert Smith, a member of the Oxford Group, who was also struggling with his alcohol addiction, and asked for a few minutes of help. The men met and talked for hours. They found a common strength in their struggle together. Wilson stayed sober. Smith had his last drink just a month after their first meeting. "Because of our kinship in suffering," Wilson wrote, "our channels of contact have always been charged with the language of the heart." Their relationship was the beginning of one of the greatest restorative organizations in the United States: Alcoholics Anonymous.[1]

Power Passage

The LORD God is a sun and shield;
    the LORD bestows favor and honor;
no good thing does he withhold
    from those whose walk is blameless.
(Psalm 84:11 NIV)

Point of Practice

The Alcoholics Anonymous organization has always had a very powerful message of confession. Wilson and Smith knew long ago, in the infancy of the group, that the only way forward was admitting where they presently were. "My name is Bill, and I'm an alcoholic," he'd say, and then the rest of the members of the group would continue. The statement was simple, but it was enough to get the ball rolling toward a place of honesty and healing.

Perhaps your struggle isn't the same as theirs. Perhaps the effects of your sin aren't as visible, but we each have some nagging sin. Remember, honesty begets healing. I have to admit I am broken before I can become whole. Confess your sins.

Consider where you are in your life today. Remember there's no true recovery without God. God is willing to do whatever you allow Him to do to help you confront your issues with the saving blood of Jesus. Recognize, admit, confess, and confront.

Point of Prayer

God, I ask that You listen to my confession. I admit my mistakes and turn over my burden for _____ to You. I now leave what belongs in the past and press toward my goals as You have taught me.

10 Pensive Points

We cannot change the past. It is one of those things in life that we just have to accept. Find a place to sit quietly and consider the years gone by. How do you feel about how you have lived your life? Are there things you've been holding on to that you need to confess to God so that you can move on?

1. What is your opinion of confession?

2. Remember one situation where you have seen the power of confession work in your life.

3. List any confessions you currently need to make to God.

4. List any confessions you currently need to make to others.

5. List any confessions you currently need to make to yourself.

6. Remember one situation where you have seen the power of confession work in the lives of others.

7. Whom do you go to converse with, and who will keep you accountable, in your moments of weakness?

8. How does confession help you find comfort and joy in your relationship with the Lord?

9. Remember when you have had a hard time admitting your struggles and ponder whether it came from feelings of denial, pride, shame, or some other emotion.

10. List three ways you can use your past or present struggles to help others who suffer from similar sins.

Power Passage

The ransomed of the LORD will return.
  They will enter Zion with singing;
    everlasting joy will crown their heads.
Gladness and joy will overtake them,
  and sorrow and sighing will flee away.
  (Isaiah 51:11 NIV)

The Spirit Daily Nourishes My Willing Soul

I am revived.

As I said earlier, I've experienced many blessings. God has been so good to me that sometimes it's overwhelming. Still, like everyone else, I have my bad days—days when I forget to say "Thank you," when it seems the struggles in life will never end and I wonder if I will ever see the light at the end of the tunnel. But despite the difficulty of my internal climb, God has shown me how to not be fatigued.

The Lord promises to nourish and restore those who actively pursue change. My relationship with the Lord has revealed to me that, while I might not know what to ask for or how to ask for it, if I'm willing to bring my sins to the table and say, "I need You," I will hear the response of the Lord.

Life is cool, life is wonderful, and life can be hard—that's the reality. We all make mistakes, no matter who we are. And God can help us through the challenges, no matter what they are, if we call on the Lord for help.

Ashley Smith was only twenty-two, fresh into life and marriage, when her life fell apart. Her husband was murdered in a knife fight. She immediately spiraled downward. In her depression, she gave up custody of her daughter and became addicted to crystal meth. For years she struggled. Her habit was debilitating, but she wanted to get better. In March 2005, after four years of addiction and three stretches in rehab, she found a new apartment and a new job. The struggle was still there, the urge to regress, but for the sake of her life and her daughter's, she was trying to give up the drug.

On the night of March 11 she was unpacking. It was two o'clock in the morning and she wanted drugs badly. She'd had some meth the night before, but she decided to settle for cigarettes. She ran out to the store to buy them and when she came back a man was sitting outside her house in a pickup truck. The man was Brian Nichols.

The TV had been playing faintly in her house all day. She'd heard the reports echo on and off, but she didn't figure it had anything to do with her. Brian Nichols had escaped from custody that morning, killing a judge, a court reporter, and a sheriff's deputy. He'd stolen a car and disappeared. He was armed and dangerous.

Brian forced Ashley inside, pushed her toward the bathroom, and tied her up. She was scared, but little by little her heart's frantic beat slowed. The man in her house was tired and lonely. He was a real person who simply wanted, like everyone else, to be understood. So instead of choosing to break down, Ashley opened up. She began talking and listening to him.

As the hours wore on, the two talked about everything from the events of the day to why Brian was in custody. They talked about being misunderstood and life's many difficult turns. Inevitably they got around to a topic of truly common ground: drugs. Brian wanted pot badly, but Ashley didn't have any. Instead she offered him what she did have: her crystal meth.

Immediately she realized her mistake. Her weakness in her struggle became more apparent to her in that moment than any moment before. While Brian wanted the drug and for Ashley to partake with him, she found a power in her life she had never had before—the power to say no.

"That moment I heard God say to me, 'Ashley, you have got to do something good for your life right now. I'm gonna give you one chance. You can do this with him, and I'm bringing you home. Because you're not gonna stop. Or you can say no and I'll let you live to help people in the world.' "

As the clock ticked on and Ashley remained a hostage, Brian continued to open up. They turned on the news and watched coverage on his murders that day. His jaw dropped. He couldn't believe what he'd done. He switched between moments of deep regret to moments of deep fear. He felt his life was over.

In the early hours of the morning, she asked if she could read to him. She pulled out her Bible and devotional and Brian listened. The words hit home. A man who had taken the lives of four people sat huddled in desperation.

By 9:00 a.m., Brian let Ashley leave the apartment to go meet her daughter. When the police came shortly thereafter, he surrendered. He waved a white shirt in the air and, for the first time that day, went peacefully.[1]

Power Passage

The Spirit helps us in our weakness. We do not know what we ought to pray for, but the Spirit himself intercedes for us with groans that words cannot express. And he who searches our hearts knows the mind of the Spirit, because the Spirit intercedes for the saints in accordance with God's will. (Romans 8:26–27 NIV)

Point of Practice

God teaches us that we can do all things through Him. Deliverance is ultimately up to us.

Despite her constant battle, Ashley was still willing to fight. She was in a Christian recovery group and daily taking her problem to the Lord. Through her persistence and His promise, delivery came when she needed it most.

For many of us, Ashley's battle is foreign. We live in a culture of immediate gratification where we've been taught we can get what we want, when we want, where we want: curbside service; twenty-four-hour grocery stores, same-day dry cleaning, drive-thru espresso. And while our society has advanced at lightning speed, our "progression" is slowly making us lose grasp of what it means to be committed and stay in something for the long haul. We take shortcuts and quick fixes instead of pursuing lasting responses to life's issues. Divorces have become automatic reflexes in marriages instead of last resorts. Surgery, instead of the treadmill, is now the answer to obesity.

Battles of the soul can't be won by pills, surgeries, or overnight deliveries. Rather than waiting until we've endured long bouts of persistence, struggle, relapse, regret, and renewal to seek help, we must meet our conflicts head-on. Issues like addiction and depression are challenges we have to meet daily. We have to wake up in the morning and make the conscious decision to move in the right direction. Like Ashley, we have to be willing to say no.

God teaches us that genuine renewal is possible. Through Him, we are given the power to truly change. As it's written in Psalm 55:22, "Cast your cares on the LORD and he will sustain you; he will never let the righteous fall" (NIV).

Jesus invites us to come to the table again and again. We don't have to struggle. With dedication and a faith in God's deliverance, we will see our lives drastically change. The truth remains: it is our responsibility to free our spirits with the Word of God!

Point of Prayer

God, I confess my sins to You. I repent for all I have done and ask Your mercy. I accept Your gift of forgiveness and look forward to this new day in hope and with the expectation of transformation in my life.

10 Pensive Points

As a Christian, you are able to ask for God's mercy and forgiveness no matter what your sin. But once you are forgiven, then what? Think about the many times you've received a second chance in life. Do you treat that grace with respect and work hard to honor the gift? Do you share it with others?

1. Think about Ashley Smith. What might have nourished her in times of her drug cravings? How did her experience enable her to so effectively communicate with Brian Nichols?

2. How can you use your stumbling blocks to serve as supports for others who struggle?

3. What has been the hardest struggle for you to overcome?

4. List the steps you have already taken to heal.

5. Next to each step on your list, note how your faith was involved in the process.

6. What do you do daily regarding your weakness to stay clear of relapse?

7. How did others support you in your weak times?

8. Think of one new thing you can do each day to allow God to nourish you.

9. How does God already daily renew your spirit?

10. Today, count the ways you tangibly see God working to nourish you.

Power Passage

If you have any encouragement from being united with Christ, if any comfort from his love, if any fellowship with the Spirit, if any tenderness and compassion, then make my joy complete by being like-minded, having the same love, being one in spirit and purpose. Do nothing out of selfish ambition or vain conceit, but in humility consider others better than yourselves. (Philippians 2:1–3 NIV)

Chapter Five

THE POWER OF PRAISE

"My fans trust me, and they trust that what I say
is true. And they also know that I'm going to be
open and honest with them about the highs, the
lows, the joys, the sorrows, but they also know
that it all ends in praise. At the end of the day
I have to go through this. We have to go
through this in order to make us better,
and in order to get to the next level."

—Yolanda[1]

God Is Most Worthy of My Praise

I make a joyful noise unto my Lord.

We are blessed to worship a giving God, a God who has generously bestowed gifts on all His children. Romans 12:6–8 says,

> We have different gifts, according to the grace given us. If a man's gift is prophesying, let him use it in proportion to his faith. If it is serving, let him serve; if it is teaching, let him teach; if it is encouraging, let him encourage; if it is contributing to the needs of others, let him give generously; if it is leadership, let him govern diligently; if it is showing mercy, let him do it cheerfully. (NIV)

I know what my purpose is in life, and I thank God for it every single day. I was put on this earth to make people aware that God is present every day. That isn't exactly what I originally had planned for myself. I graduated from Texas Southern University in 1984 with a degree in journalism. I was looking forward to a future as a broadcaster. I had visions of *The Evening News with Yolanda Adams*.

God had other plans. My boss at the station where I had interned and was planning to work was replaced, and with him went my chances for what I thought was going to be my career.

I was very disappointed; in fact I was crushed, but I never lost my faith. I never stopped praising God for all He had done for me and for what I knew the Holy Spirit would continue to do. Even though things didn't go as I thought they should, I was certain God had something else bigger and better in mind for me.

I like to think of the Lord as what I call an everyday God. You won't find the Holy Spirit only in a church, in a tabernacle, or in a cathedral. God walks with us every day, everywhere we go. You can talk to God. You can have a relationship with the Lord. The Holy Spirit is real.

When things didn't work out in television broadcasting, I followed God's path to teaching and loved it. I taught for a few years and continued to praise the Lord and to listen for God's voice during that time. It turns out I wasn't supposed to continue teaching in a classroom but rather from stages and concert halls around the world. God wanted me to teach through song, to make people aware of God's presence around them all the time. God wanted me to talk to people about what I had learned, so the Lord blessed me with a radio show. The Lord wanted me to share that God is the best friend we will ever have, and we can live our lives as a testament to the Lord's goodness.

We can show gratitude for all the Lord has done for us and all that God will do for us in the way we conduct ourselves. We praise God in the way we live. The way I treat my family and friends is how I praise God. Being a great and engaged mother is how I praise God. My radio show is how I praise God. My music is about praising God. I write songs that praise the Lord; I sing songs that praise God. God's Word is so powerful I see it as my job to spread it. I know this is part of the Lord's plan for me.

Do you understand what I am saying? *Everything* I do is about praising God. The purpose of my life is to praise the Lord, no matter what is happening at the time.

What is your purpose? What is your gift? Find it. Then embrace it, pursue it, practice it, whatever it is. Thank God for everything that comes your way. Thank the Lord for all you are going to have. Make your life a joyful noise until the Lord, even if it doesn't look like what you think it should, even if you don't understand all that is happening. Don't just talk about your love for the Lord, show God your praise!

Carla Harris knows about praising God. When she was a senior at Bishop Kenny High School in Jacksonville, Florida, and thinking about college, she was advised not to apply to any Ivy League schools. They would be expensive and hard to get into. Always motivated by someone telling her she couldn't do something, she applied anyway. She was accepted to three Ivy League schools, and one of them was Harvard.

Her mother, Billie, a schoolteacher, and her father, a commercial fishing boat captain and later a retail business owner, had struggled just to pay the yearly tuition at Bishop Kenny and had no idea how they would pay for an expensive Harvard education. But this devout family trusted God, praised the Lord for offering Carla this wonderful opportunity and all the others the Holy Spirit would send to her in her life, and they found a way. That was not the first or last time life handed Carla Harris a mountain to climb over.

When she was a freshman, one of her professors told her she wouldn't do well in economics. Carla, being Carla, decided to major in economics. With her only business experience a job working at McDonald's, she then applied for a summer internship to work in finance. She told the interviewer how the job had helped her develop selling, customer service, and execution skills. She got the internship through the Sponsors for Educational Opportunity

(SEO) program and then landed a job at Blyth Eastman Paine Webber. She went on to land a full-time job at one of the world's premier investment banks, Morgan Stanley, after graduation.

The early part of her career on Wall Street was no closer to smooth sailing. Carla watched her colleagues' careers jet ahead while hers felt stuck, and she once worked with a boss who she felt was intent on ruining her confidence and self-esteem. But through those and many other struggles up the career ladder, Carla's praise for God never faltered. "I know who I am, and whose I am," Carla said in a recent speech. She gives motivational talks around the country trying to help other professionals navigate the sometimes choppy waters of the corporate world. "I know that I wouldn't enjoy any of the blessings I have in my life without God. The Lord is at the center of everything I do."

Like all of us, Carla has bad days, but whenever she does she says she simply reminds herself: "I can do all things through Christ." Carla says, "Everything I do is from that spiritual base. No matter what happens I have the courage to act, stand up for what is right, take risks, or do whatever else I need to. I give God all the praise. I know the Lord is always with me, so there is nothing to fear.

"I am not always successful in everything I try to do, but I still praise God, even for my failures, because I learn from them and gain valuable experience. Everything is a gift from God." Carla's life is about faith and praising God for all life offers us, good and seemingly not so good. "You have to stick to your faith because you can't foresee the outcomes in life, only God knows the plan. I just continue praising God no matter what happens, and I know the Lord will bring me everything I desire."

Today Carla is one of the first African American women to become a managing director on Wall Street. She has received numerous honors and awards including being named to Fortune's list of "The 50 Most Powerful Black Executives in America," and Black Enterprise's "50 Most Powerful Women in Business." She puts her gifts and business acumen to use by serving on countless nonprofit boards and with a variety of charities.

In addition to her business success, Carla also has a gift for singing and loves to perform gospel music. She sings in her church choir and donates all of the proceeds from her CDs and concerts, which include two performances at New York City's famed Carnegie Hall, to her alma mater Bishop Kenny and to St. Charles Borromeo School in Harlem. She has raised thousands of dollars to support scholarships for African American students. No matter what the situation, Carla's motto is always "God is good all the time!"[1]

Power Passage

I will extol the LORD at all times;
    his praise will always be on my lips.
My soul will boast in the LORD;
    let the afflicted hear and rejoice.
Glorify the LORD with me;
    let us exalt his name together.
(Psalm 34:1–3 NIV)

Point of Practice

Life doesn't always work out the way we think it should. But when we have the courage to continue to follow God's plan without anger and resentment but with a spirit of joy, openness, and expectation, giving God the praise for the good we do have, the Lord will expose opportunities and dormant gifts we had no idea existed. God created us to be perpetual manufacturers; we should always be active doing and producing, thanking the Lord for the gifts we have and using them to make the world around us a better place. We never use all the power within us. God has built us to persevere. He did not create us for sloth or complacency but for glory.

While we pursue dreams, we must be careful to make sure those dreams are in tune with the desires of God. We have to ask ourselves if we are showing God the praise for what He has brought us in life or if we are charging full speed ahead with tunnel vision. It's essential to listen to wisdom and be open to change. In my life, the best things have always come unexpectedly—things I never planned or never would have asked for. But we are blessed to have a Father who knows what's best for us, and if we stay faithful in our praise of the Lord, we will enjoy a bounty of gifts in our lives that is beyond our imagination.

Hebrews 10:22–23 says, "Let us draw near to God with a sincere heart in full assurance of faith, having our hearts sprinkled to cleanse us from a guilty conscience and having our bodies washed with pure water. Let us hold unswervingly to the hope we profess, for he who promised is faithful" (NIV). If you follow God's plan instead of your own, you will find your course altered. If you believe in the promises of God, if you continue to praise the Lord and root yourself in His faithfulness, you can move forward with the knowledge that He has designed a more beautiful life for you than you could have ever planned yourself.

Carla certainly never imagined she'd be one of the most powerful women on Wall Street, or that she'd find herself standing on the stage singing at Carnegie Hall. Think about your gifts and goals. What dreams could you be missing out on because you are not willing to give the Lord praise when things aren't going as you think they should?

Point of Prayer

God, for every trial I've had to face, for every challenge I've had to overcome, for every mountain I've had to speak to, I know that I am growing in knowledge and faith of Your love and omniscient presence, and for all this I give You praise.

10 Pensive Points

Life is full of twists and turns. The unexpected is just as likely to occur as the expected. Think about how you praise God. Do you praise the Lord under all circumstances? Or do you reserve your praise of the Holy Spirit for only when things go your way?

1. List the promises of God you already believe in and for which you already praise God.

2. What is one important goal you have? Name one thing you do to praise God in light of that goal.

3. God will sometimes take us off our planned paths. When that happens, do you whine and complain, or do you look for the gift?

4. Was there a time when things didn't go your way? Can you name an unexpected gift that resulted from the situation?

5. Think about ways you could work to become a better listener for God's plan. Write down three ideas and read them every morning before you begin your day.

6. Praising God for the opportunities in life requires courage and faith. In what ways are you willing to take the brave steps to walk the path of God's plan for your life?

7. Are there people whose lives you admire, who are strong in their faith? What things do they do to live a faithful life?

Do you know someone whose life course has been altered from his or her chosen path for the better?

8. Carla had quite a few people in her life tell her she couldn't do things. Do you listen when someone tells you something is impossible? Or do you believe, as she does, that with Christ all things are possible?

9. Find a piece of art or some other physical object that reminds you to praise God for all of your gifts. Put it someplace where you will see it often.

10. What are some ways you could show thanks and praise God every day for what you have in your life right now?

Power Passage

I will praise you forever for what you have done;
> in your name I will hope, for your name is good.
I will praise you in the presence of your saints.
> (Psalm 52:9 NIV)

God Always Shepherds Me to Full Pastures

I trust God's faithful guidance.

I am one of those people who plans, plans, plans. When I die they will probably write on my tombstone: "Here lies Yolanda Adams; she had plans." But sometimes my plans are just that—my plans—and I stop just short of making sure I see them through to fruition. I get frazzled and distracted and then, just when I am about to reach my goal, I skip over some seemingly minor detail that derails everything. For example, I might plan for weeks to go to an early appointment. The night before the meeting, I fall into bed and then suddenly remember that I forgot to put the directions to where I have to go in my purse.

The next morning, in my haste I get up, get dressed, rush out, and start driving down the road, but after a few minutes I realize I have no idea where I am going. I may have had a plan, but when a voice told me the night before that there was one other thing I needed to do, that I needed to get up and put those directions in my bag, that I had missed an important step, I decided, *No, I've got it covered, I can do it my way.*

The same happens on the road of life. We make elaborate plans for things but decide, just as we are about to be victorious, just as God steps in to help us over the finish line, we've got it covered. Even though we hear God's voice whisper, "You'd better take care of that," we decide, *No, I can skip that step*. We decide we are too busy to do it God's way, and we are going to do it our way because it's easier.

Rather than give God the praise for His all-knowing wisdom, we ignore the tooth that hurts just a little instead of making the dentist appointment. We know we should call the plumber, but instead we let the bathroom leak go for another week. Rather than stopping at the gas station, we ignore the flashing light on the dashboard. And then the inevitable happens. The uncomfortable tooth turns into a toothache, the leak turns into a flood, and the car conks out on the highway. Rather than giving God the praise for knowing the plan, instead of listening to the Lord's instructions designed to help us, we let our egos lead the way.

When I catch myself doing this, I just laugh out loud. I say, "Yolanda! Stop it! You know better!" I stop, as I did that day when I was miles from home without my directions. I pull off the road, look up, and say, "Okay, God, I am sorry. Thank You for reminding me. I praise Your name. I praise You." I sigh and ask the Lord to forgive me yet again. I ask for a calmer spirit and better listening skills, and then I ask for help in figuring out where I need to go! I pick up the phone and call someone who can give me directions. As wonderful as we think our ideas are, they are never as wonderful as God's.

Scripture tells the story of when God's people needed to trust His plan. In Egypt, the days of Joseph had passed. The old pharaoh had died and a new king had come to reign. The Israelites, who had grown in number and in strength, were gradually being crushed under the thumb of the new Egyptian kings. For four hundred years, they were bottled up in the mass misery of slavery, building brick by brick a new Egypt that they would not be able to call their own. In their oppression and bondage, they cried out. They asked God for rescue and He heard their pleas, granting them deliverance via the hands of two unlikely men: Moses and Aaron.

After being called by God, the two men approached Pharaoh, offering the Lord's request to let the Hebrews go. But Pharaoh saw them as his own property and didn't respect the authority of God. "Who is the LORD," he said, "that I should obey him and let Israel go? I do not know the LORD and I will not let Israel go" (Exodus 5:2 NIV).

His ignorance and defiance cost him greatly. The Lord sent plagues upon Egypt: blood, frogs, gnats, flies, dead livestock, boils, hail, locusts, and darkness. But Pharaoh still would not let the people go. It wasn't until the tenth plague—death of all the first-born sons—that Pharaoh's heart grew weary and he conceded to God's power, saying, "Up! Leave my people, you and the Israelites! Go, worship the LORD as you have requested" (Exodus 12:31 NIV).

Yet after the Hebrews packed up and left, Pharaoh forgot the hardships his people had endured and remembered only the labor he was losing. He got six hundred of his best chariots ready, assembled his army, and pursued his fleeing slaves.

By the time Pharaoh and his men had reached them, the Israelites were standing in front of the Red Sea. With the army fast approaching, the situation looked hopeless. The Israelites questioned, but Moses remained faithful. "Do not be afraid," he said. "Stand firm and you will see the deliverance the LORD will bring you today. The Egyptians you see today you will never see again. The LORD will fight for you; you need only to be still" (Exodus 14:13–14 NIV). Then he raised his staff and parted the Red Sea for the Hebrew people to cross on foot without boats. The Egyptians, eager for victory, pursued them, but after the Israelites had passed to the other side, the waters returned and swallowed the Egyptian army.

Power Passage

Thanks be to God, who always leads us in triumphal procession in Christ and through us spreads everywhere the fragrance of the knowledge of him. (2 Corinthians 2:14 NIV)

Point of Practice

What seems to be impossible is always possible for God. When we have faith in the Lord and listen for God's guidance, we will always be led onward to the right path of destiny.

The story of Israel's deliverance is a symbol of God's deliverance in our own lives. All people are shackled with their own sins, slave to their faults and transgressions. Burdened by our weaknesses, we can't rely on ourselves. We need God.

Psalm 91:14–16 says,

> "Because he loves me," says the LORD,
> "I will rescue him;
> I will protect him, for he acknowledges my name.
> He will call upon me, and I will answer him;
> I will be with him in trouble,
> I will deliver him and honor him.
> With long life will I satisfy him
> and show him my salvation." (NIV)

As Christians, we must trust in the promise of rescue and give praise for His faithful deliverance. We worship a God of divine guidance, and we can move forward in the assurance that He's always with us.

Point of Prayer

God, I know You know best. Please help me remember that Your way is always the best way. Lead me down the path You think is best, and I will faithfully follow.

10 Pensive Points

Following God's voice and remaining steadfast in our praise is not always easy. We hear the Lord's voice and decide that our way is better. Still, in order to live the life God has planned for us, we must be able to discern the Lord's voice and plans from our own.

1. Can you relate to Pharaoh's struggle with listening to the Lord?

2. Discerning God's voice isn't always easy. What are some ways you can listen better for the Lord's guidance?

3. Think about a recent struggle you had. List three ways you could have praised God's plan and followed it instead of your own.

4. Would you have had the courage to follow Moses' instructions at the Red Sea? What ways have you stepped out in a direction that you weren't sure of? How did things turn out?

5. Moses was a man of tremendous strength. If God had called you to liberate such a people, would you have had faith in the Lord and followed the call? Would you have been able to follow through?

6. List five reasons God deserves praise for things He has done in your life this week alone.

7. What situations in the past has God guided you out of? How did you know it was the Lord's path and not yours?

8. Write down at least one way you have asked for help this week.

9. When you chose your own path, how did the end results compare to when you chose to trust in and praise God?

10. List ways you already faithfully follow God's instructions in your life.

Power Passage

The God of all grace, who called you to his eternal glory in Christ, after you have suffered a little while, will himself restore you and make you strong, firm and steadfast. To him be the power for ever and ever. Amen. (1 Peter 5:10–11 NIV)

I Am Rich in the Grace of God

His grace is like overflowing water.

I think of my life as a kind of constant praise song for God. God is in everything I do and every decision I make. To me God is like water: the Lord flows everywhere, and just as you can't live without water, you can't live without God. If you are thirsty, all you need to do is drink from the Lord's cup and you will be satisfied. I praise the Holy Spirit for everything in my life. Songs like "Thank You, Lord" exemplify how I feel about God. The gratitude for all the Lord has done comes from deep within me and comes out in my music.

I praise God with enthusiasm and gusto. I can't praise the Lord enough! I get so emotional about it sometimes; I am often overwhelmed by the countless blessings in my life. It's an awesome responsibility that God has given me. I want people to see how amazing God is and understand what the Lord can do if they believe. When I sing I pray that God lets me be the best example of what the Lord wants to say in the song, what God wants people to hear. People see me on the stage in my beautiful clothes, they hear my voice, but that's just the package the message comes in. It's not about me at all; it's about delivering the message of the Holy Spirit. I am just the vessel. The Lord gets all the praise.

God's Word and truth are our salvation; as water is to our body's health, they are the true means of spiritual nourishment. When we learn the joy of spiritual fulfillment we are fully satisfied. Come to the well of God, drink often and deeply from it, and you will finally learn what it means to be filled.

Jesus was on a long journey. Traveling from Judea to Galilee, He stopped in Samaria at a town called Sychar. He was resting by a well when a Samaritan woman came for water. Jesus asked her for a drink. The woman was taken aback. Jews never associated with Samaritans. To acknowledge her at all seemed unbelievable. In her shock, she asked Jesus why He would approach her.

Jesus wasn't concerned that she was a Samaritan. He was tired and parched, but He knew the woman had the greatest thirst. "If you knew the gift of God and who it is that asks you for a drink, you would have asked him and he would have given you living water," He said, breaking another convention by conversing with a woman (John 4:10 NIV).

The woman was an outcast. She had already had five husbands and was then living with a man she was not married to. She was deep in sin. She realized her desperate need for help and asked to be filled. "Sir, give me this water so that I won't get thirsty and have to keep coming here to draw water" (John 4:15 NIV). In His infinite grace, Jesus answered her call and filled her cup.

Power Passage

"My grace is sufficient for you, for my power is made perfect in weakness." Therefore, I will boast all the more gladly about my weaknesses, so that Christ's power may rest on me. (2 Corinthians 12:9 NIV)

Point of Practice

I love the story of the Samaritan woman at the well. I often preach about her. She finally found someone who had real answers. His name was Jesus.

The Samaritan woman was in the deepest rut. She didn't trust any longer in the potential for her life. Many of us feel the same way. We become so familiar with our depravity that we don't know who we are without it.

The promise of the living God is the promise of redemption. Just as Jesus was at the well offering the woman pure truth that refreshes and renews, He is offering it to us. He will quench our thirst and nourish us in ways we couldn't even imagine.

Point of Prayer

God, I come to the well of Your goodness and love to replenish my soul and my spirit. I drink from Your never-ending fountain of blessings and move forward in my life with the richness of Your grace. I let Your love fill me like the vastness of the ocean, cool me like an ice-cold glass of water on a summer's day, and renew me as a spring rain nourishes the flowers and trees into bloom.

10 Pensive Points

We forget how plentiful God's blessings are. All it takes to start a relationship with God is simply to start the flow, to turn on the faucet. Just as you would drink a cup of water and let it refresh your body, you can take God into your spirit and let the Lord begin to renew your life.

1. Can you sympathize with the woman at the well? Are there places in your life where you have lost your faith?

2. What are you really thirsty for?

3. What people or things in your life are you using to fill yourself up? How do you feel after you turn to them?

4. Consider ways God's Word could be substituted for those people or things.

5. God offers us grace whenever we ask for it. We can come to the well at any time. What is stopping you from coming to the well of the Lord?

6. Are there people in your life who seem full of God's promise? List some things about them that you'd like to emulate in your own life.

7. Choose someone you admire, and talk to him or her about God's grace in his or her life. Did you learn anything about this person that surprised you?

8. Like the woman at the well, are you willing to ask the Lord for a drink?

9. Imagine your life full of grace and promise, fresh and new. What does it look like?

10. What steps can you take right now to make that life a reality?

Power Passage

"Surely God is my salvation;
    I will trust and not be afraid.
The Lord, the Lord, is my strength and my song;
    he has become my salvation."
With joy you will draw water
    from the wells of salvation. (Isaiah 12:2–3 NIV)

I Give Thanks in All Circumstances

I have blessings in disguise.

Sometimes it's difficult to look through pain and see potential blessings ahead. But God has a divine plan. He has shown me that while we might not always understand His plans and His goals, throughout our lives He faithfully guides us to places of fulfillment and purpose.

I never expected to be a single mom. When I married for the second time I was certain it would be forever. There are people who don't agree, but I know that my marriage was meant to be for a season. My ex-husband is a wonderful person and we are both doing our best to raise a healthy, happy daughter who loves Jesus. It isn't always easy, but I praise God even for these circumstances. I know that the Lord's bigger plan is at work.

God is so awesome! He even allows us to see the good in life while experiencing tough times. God's plans for your life are always to give you hope and a future! Trust in the Lord and give thanks in all circumstances. Rest in Him.

Randy Pausch was only forty-five when he was diagnosed with

pancreatic cancer. By his last months, ten tumors burdened his liver. Daily he weakened, and it was visible in his face and shrinking frame. He was going to leave behind three children, a wife, and all the dreams he'd never realize. But he knew feeling bad for himself wouldn't do any good. Joy shone in his eyes. "We don't beat the reaper by living longer," he said. "We beat the reaper by living well and living fully."

Randy Pausch was a family man and a university man. He received his bachelor's in computer science from Brown and his doctorate from Carnegie Mellon. He went on to teach computer science at Carnegie Mellon for ten years, eventually cofounding a master's degree program that bridged the artistic and engineering worlds. He was heavily involved with the lives of his students, constantly inspiring them. When he found out about the cancer, his investment in the lives of those he was leaving didn't slacken. He knew he had more to say.

After a year of living with cancer and receiving the diagnosis that he had three to six months left of good health, Randy Pausch gave his last lecture called "Really Achieving Your Childhood Dreams." To an audience of roughly four hundred, he spoke humorously and candidly about the decisions we have as human beings to embrace our dreams and the attitudes we take to achieve those aims. "Each of us must make a decision," he said, "to be a fun-loving Tigger or a sad-sack Eeyore."

Pausch left his mark. Expounding on the lecture he gave at Carnegie Mellon, he published *The Last Lecture*, a book that quickly became a number one best seller. More than six million people have downloaded and watched the lecture that defines Pausch's positive outlook in the face of pain. "If I don't seem as depressed or morose as I should be," he said, "sorry to disappoint you. . . . I'm dying and I'm having fun."

Despite his faith and good humor, the cancer was unbeatable.

Pausch died, leaving behind his three children, his wife, and his legacy of inspiration.[1]

Power Passage

We do not lose heart. Though outwardly we are wasting away, yet inwardly we are being renewed day by day. For our light and momentary troubles are achieving for us an eternal glory that far outweighs them all. So we fix our eyes not on what is seen, but on what is unseen. For what is seen is temporary, but what is unseen is eternal. (2 Corinthians 4:16–18 NIV)

Point of Practice

Some people would say that Randy died too soon. But God used him to touch millions upon millions of people. He took control of his life until the end! He lived, loved, and celebrated with everything in him.

We are blessed to learn Pausch's lesson on a small scale. While some of us have dealt with disease, most of our pain comes from other areas of life. Like Pausch, we should ask ourselves what we can do with our reality and whom we can empower. Even the gravest circumstances have potential. God calls us, as followers of Christ, to give thanks in all circumstances. He challenges us to open our eyes wide in the worst of situations and look for Him. *There is beauty in the heartbreak*, He assures us. *I will use your deepest hurts for the greatest good.*

Point of Prayer

God, I know my time on earth is precious. The next moment is not guaranteed. Help me, Lord, make the best of every day. Help me celebrate the gift of life even when things are challenging. Help me see and share the good You have given me with everyone I come into contact with every day. Thank You for the blessings of my life, God. I am grateful.

10 Pensive Points

We know that life will bring us challenges, but how we approach them is evidence of our true belief in God's Word. The Lord used Randy to teach the world that if we choose to, we can find ways to be thankful for our lives and praise God for our blessings under any circumstances.

1. Put yourself in Randy's shoes. If you were diagnosed with a fatal cancer, do you believe you could continue to praise God?

2. What were some of the good things that came from Randy's circumstances?

3. Imagine you were given six months to live. What five things would you do to show the world the good God has done in your life?

4. How does your response to that question align with how you are living today?

5. Write down five things you would want your family or friends to know about God if you were going to die tomorrow.

6. Look back at some of the most difficult moments of your life. In hindsight, were there any hidden blessings? What good did God give you from the difficult situation?

7. Consider a painful or difficult situation you are currently facing. How could you turn it around? Can you locate God's good in it?

8. For the next week, before you go to bed, list at least five things you have to be thankful to God for from the day. At the end of the seven days notice how you feel.

9. What do you need to do to incorporate thanks to God into your life every day?

10. Think of one way you can share the goodness of God with someone in your life today. Go and do it.

Power Passage

Be joyful always; pray continually; give thanks in all circumstances, for this is God's will for you in Christ Jesus. (1 Thessalonians 5:16–18 NIV)

p.

Chapter Six

THE POWER OF CONFIDENT ASSURANCE

⌘

"Blessed assurance, Jesus is mine!
O what a foretaste of glory divine!"

—*Fanny J. Crosby* [1]

Every Promise Is God-Breathed

My God is continually faithful.

On the road to an abundant life we will meet doubters—those who pepper our faith with tiny bits of skepticism. If we allow it, their words of discouragement can stunt our belief. God created us to be valiant human beings. He wants us to be challenged and to pursue life vigorously. In "Open Your Heart" I sing about letting God's will be done in my life. My job is to faithfully follow the Lord's words and directions without doubting or questioning the Holy Spirit. There is no place for fear or doubt when you have faith in God. The Lord has your back. Whatever you are facing, God has it covered. You can rest in that assurance every day and therefore continue on in life with enthusiasm and purpose, without concern for what others might think or say.

Not everyone understands or even likes who I am or what I do as an artist. They don't like that I experiment with mixing gospel and secular sounds, traditional and modern music. They don't like that some of my songs have dance mix versions, or that I sometimes perform and collaborate with nongospel artists. But because I trust that God gave me a gift to share with the world, I have the courage to keep walking down the path, because I know God is right there with me. I want the whole world to hear God's message, and that's what I focus on. I have a ministry to share, and some of the people who really need to hear the message aren't in a church or the other traditional places gospel music is played. So in order to act out God's plan for my life, I have to meet people where they are.

God promises us abundant life. God's promises are ever-flowing and never-ceasing. Every one of God's promises builds faith. Every one of God's promises removes doubt. The Lord knows our ability to reach our destination. With the support of a continually merciful, faithful God, we can move confidently ahead, knowing God is taking every step with us.

Billy Graham was born in 1918, four days after World War I ended; he was raised in a family of pious persistence. On a dairy farm with plenty of biblical and moral rearing, he had a typical childhood and adolescence. He wanted to be a baseball star.

But in 1934, at age sixteen, his dream changed. He heard the preaching of Mordecai Ham, an evangelist whose ministry made pit stops through Graham's hometown of Charlotte, North Carolina. "I didn't have any tears, I didn't have any emotion, I didn't hear any thunder, there was no lightning," he said. "But right there, I made my decision to live my life for Christ. It was as simple as that, and as conclusive."

After high school, Graham went to Tennessee to Bob Jones College, a religious institute known for its severe conservatism. Graham was an outsider. He couldn't align his beliefs with theirs. Even though his fellow students and professors didn't agree, he knew his approach to God was the right one for him. His heart was still in the gospel. Rather than try to contort his thinking to fit, he stayed faithful to his beliefs. He left Tennessee and headed to the Florida Bible Institute, where he found like-minded people and felt more at home.

In Florida, Graham became devoted to the practice of preaching. Standing in lone canoes on solitary lakes, he would spout the gospel into the air. He would conduct sermons to the only audiences he could find—squirrels and stray animals. He would linger outside bars known for their drunkards and debauchery, sharing words of truth with souls who seemed lost and empty. At the time he seemed like a nice boy who might one day, if he were lucky, preach consistently someplace to a small congregation. His words were powerful. His sermons were unique. But no one thought that this tall, lanky farm boy with a sincere demeanor would eventually become an orator to thousands.

In 1940, Graham left Florida. He received a scholarship to Wheaton College in Illinois and moved north to further his education. It was in Wheaton that he met Ruth Bell, the woman who would become his wife. It was Ruth who would eventually encourage him to pursue the career that would change his life and the lives of millions of others.

After graduation and marriage, Graham began his long life in evangelism. Starting with Youth for Christ International, he joined other young preachers who were bringing a new face and voice to a gospel that had lost its grasp on the emerging generation. The younger audience brought a sense of modernity to the church, yet Graham was committed to the moral truths of the Bible. In a small hotel room in California, Graham and the other preachers committed to the Modesto Manifesto, a pledge that would make their lives transparent to the skeptical public. They would be entirely open about finances; they wouldn't spend time alone with any women but their wives. Via the Modesto Manifesto, they hoped to prevent misunderstanding and avoid human failings that might prevent others from receiving the gospel.

After his time with Youth for Christ International, Graham saw his audience grow. In 1949, his legacy was established at the Los Angeles crusade, an event that lasted eight weeks with circus tents on pavement filled to capacity, new believers spilling over and out into the city streets. Other crusades maintained the same vivacity. In London, he ran for twelve weeks. In New York, sixteen. Still, not everyone was a fan. Some criticized Graham and accused him of setting religion back one hundred years. But Graham was undaunted. He is reported to have replied, "I did indeed want to set religion back, not just 100 years but 1,900 years, to the Book of Acts, when first-century followers of Christ were accused of turning the Roman Empire upside down."

Since that time, the Graham family has become known as the royal family of American religion. With more than sixty years in Christian ministry, Billy has published more than twenty-five books, counseled numerous American presidents, received an honorary knighthood, been named one of the ten most admired men in the world, and has preached to more than two million people in nearly two hundred countries. The unlikely farm boy with dreams of baseball diamonds has led many to Christ.[1]

Power Passage

> If the LORD delights in a man's way,
>> he makes his steps firm;
> though he stumble, he will not fall,
>> for the LORD upholds him with his hand.
>> (Psalm 37:23–24 NIV)

Point of Practice

I've known and loved the Graham family for many years. The Grahams clearly love God, they love people, and they walk the Word. Although Dr. Graham had a well-thought-out plan, God had a bigger and better one! Today Billy Graham's name is synonymous with ministry. His authentic voice has wakened millions to the calling of Christ.

But Billy's life didn't start out that way. People doubted his ability and doubted his method. In a profession of studied intellectuals, Graham walked in the truth of the Word he knew. With persistence and a belief in the Lord's calling, Graham was able to shut out the doubts of the skeptics and vigorously pursue his greater calling. He knew every promise was God-breathed, and he was in the hands of the continually faithful.

As with Graham, our dreams and pursuits come head-to-head with skeptics, people who will naysay and scowl at our greatest ambitions. But God doesn't give us anything we can't handle. God is faithful. "I tell you the truth, if anyone says to this mountain, 'Go, throw yourself into the sea,' and does not doubt in his heart but believes that what he says will happen, it will be done for him" (Mark 11:23 NIV).

When others doubt us, they are only saying they don't believe in the great promises of God. They want us to believe that He is faithful only to a degree, only when our requests are simple and our needs easily met. But do not let your knees buckle under the unbelieving assumptions of others. He who is faithful will provide a way for you to stand up with conviction and understanding.

Trust God in the uncertainties of life. No matter how unfortunate circumstances may seem, remember, God is sovereign. So believe God!

Point of Prayer

God, my faith in Your Word and Your way is strong and unwavering. I walk forward in my life knowing that You are always with me, guiding my way.

10 Pensive Points

When we are on God's path, not everyone is going to encourage and support us. In fact, many people will try to detour us from our destiny. Part of having faith is knowing who you are in God's eyes and walking toward your goals no matter what people say.

1. Can you relate to the story of Billy Graham? Were you surprised to learn how he started out?

2. Have you ever found yourself surrounded by people who didn't believe you could succeed? How did that make you feel? Did it stop you?

3. Have you ever gone against the crowd? What was the outcome?

4. List three things you've always wanted to do but haven't yet accomplished.

5. Make a list of the people you spend most of your time with. Put them in two categories: supporters and skeptics. Which column is longer?

6. Are there people in your life who are impacting your belief in yourself in a negative way? Do you need to let go of those relationships?

7. Think about your role in the lives of your friends and family. Are you a support beam or a source of doubt?

8. How can you help foster a sense of belief in others who likewise doubt their true callings and abilities?

9. Think about your experiences. How has God already been continually faithful in your life?

10. List three ways you can step out this week toward some long-held goal you have been putting off in your life.

Power Passage

This is the message we have heard from him and declare to you: God is light; in him there is no darkness at all. (1 John 1:5 NIV)

I Am Blessed Because the Lord Guides My Way

The Lord divines my steps.

Every morning we wake up to endless possibilities. We have choices to make. We can begin with hope, anticipation, and optimism, or we can begin with despair, despondency, and pessimism.

Living with confidence in the Lord, we have the ability and blessing to claim every hour to its fullest and pursue every dream to its heights. Life has its ups and downs. There are days when I feel inspired and other days when I want to just throw in the towel. I sing about that in my song "Day by Day." Every day, good or not so good, I call on God for strength. I reach out to the Lord in prayer and meditation and ask to feel the Holy Spirit's presence as I go about my day. I place my trust in God and know that I can go with confidence and show the world that I am a child of God in all I say and do.

Terms like "impossible" and "too difficult" burden our vocabulary when the truth is that God is constantly and carefully guiding our way. Life is a process. Once you decide you want God to lead you in your life, when you come up against the hard stuff, you call on the Lord, ask for help and guidance, and then keep working. It doesn't happen overnight—you don't just fly off into God's glory like some kind of superhero. You put one foot in front of the other and take it, as the song says, day by day.

Learn to trust in Him, and you will live a life that has been beautifully tailored to fit you perfectly. Never forget how wonderful and beautiful each day is. Choose to love yourself! Choose to forget the past but, most importantly, choose to have confidence in God!

The New Testament is filled with stories of doubt dissolved by faith. Countless times God shows His strength, mercy, and dominion through the actions of His Son, Jesus Christ, assuring the doubting multitudes of His true identity. But I think one of the greatest instances of such assurance is found in the few small steps Peter took on the water.

After the feeding of the five thousand, Jesus sent His disciples back to the boat to cross the Sea of Galilee. The crowd dispersed and He went up on the mountain to pray. He needed time alone to contemplate and talk with the Father. By the time He came down from the mountain, it was already night and darkness had fallen over the water. With the weight of the wind, the boat carrying the group was already a great distance from land. Instead of calling the disciples back, Jesus simply walked out to them, His steps as sure on the liquid water as they were on the solid land.

While the disciples had seen Jesus perform miracles countless times, they were still in awe of the figure approaching them. They assumed it was a ghost and they were terrified. But Jesus assured them of His presence: "Take courage! It is I. Don't be afraid" (Matthew 14:27 NIV).

"Lord, if it's you," Peter replied, "tell me to come to you on the water" (14:28 NIV).

Jesus called Peter to Him. With his eyes fixed on the Lord, Peter miraculously stepped out onto the water and began walking to Jesus. But within a few steps, Peter got distracted by the wind and the waves raging around him; he took his eyes off Jesus and his confidence weakened. He began to sink and cried out for help. Jesus reached out immediately and caught him, asking the eternal question asked of all believers: "You of little faith, why did you doubt?" (Matthew 14:31 NIV). Together they got back into the boat. The water and wind around them subsided.

Power Passage

The lot is cast into the lap,
    but its every decision is from the LORD.
    (Proverbs 16:33 NIV)

Point of Practice

Wow! How many times have we been Peter? His story is one of doubt meeting faith.

When Jesus stood out on the water, Peter knew it was the Lord. He called out to Jesus and asked Him to challenge his faith. Jesus called him out of his place of comfort to where it was unfamiliar and scary. He asked Peter to take a risk.

With confidence in God and his eyes locked on Jesus, Peter stepped out of the boat. One foot after the other, he walked on a surface that normally would have swallowed him. But when the wind came, Peter remembered where he was. He focused on the impossible nature of what was occurring. With his confidence transferred to himself rather than God, he began to sink.

Peter lost faith for a moment, and Jesus saved him quickly. When we align ourselves with the Lord and focus on His promises, we are able to do incredible things. Faith is our confident assurance of God, who never promised our way would be easy or simple. He just promised it would be worthwhile, that God's Spirit would be with us. Our comfort zone in life should always be the presence of God! God offers us great promises if we are willing to take great risks. Faith in God means believing there is more to life than we can experience on our own. He has designed our steps and given us the ability to walk on water. If we're willing to trust Him and believe in His truths above our doubts, we will be able to step out of our insecurities into the beauty of His promises.

Point of Prayer

God, I may not always be able to see You, but I know You are there. Order my steps, Lord, and give me the courage to follow Your plan. I praise You for all You have done and for all You are about to do in my life.

10 Pensive Points

Though we may not literally have to walk across water, we will go through challenging, difficult, faith-testing circumstances. Like Peter, we will face things we think we cannot do. Are you sinking into despair, or are you looking to Jesus and His miraculous power for guidance in your life?

1. Reread Matthew 14:22–36. What gave Peter confidence?
2. How did Peter demonstrate great faith even before he stepped out onto the water?
3. Think of one thing that gives you faith today.
4. In what small ways can you demonstrate faith before taking a big risk?
5. How did Peter differ from the disciples in the boat? Are you more like Peter or those who stayed in the boat?

6. What is your boat?

7. What big risk is God calling you to take?

8. Write down what you believe is possible if you're willing to step out.

9. What could distract you from achieving that possibility?

10. Jesus asks Peter the important question: "Why did you doubt?" How would you respond to this question?

Power Passage

He who began a good work in you will carry it on to completion until the day of Christ Jesus. (Philippians 1:6 NIV)

Life and Death Are in My Tongue

My mouth controls my destiny.

Words matter. You can lift someone's day by saying, "Good morning," "I am glad to see you," "What a pretty outfit," or giving some other compliment. Words have the power to inspire, to give hope, to encourage, and to comfort. Are there any three sweeter words on the planet than "I love you"? Whether they come from a friend, your soul mate, or your mom, the power in those three little words is undeniable. Words can change your life.

Just as words can build us up, they can also break us down. Think about how bad you feel when someone speaks to you using angry, hurtful, or untrue words. Just as words of love can lift you, angry, ugly words can break you down, make you sad or depressed.

I am so humbled when fans approach me or take the time to write or e-mail to let me know that the lyrics of one of my songs touched their lives:

> Yolanda's music has been there for me in good times as well as bad. Through her music, she lets you know that you are not alone.[1]

Her music touches my heart and soul. My mother passed away July 17, 2000, and Yolanda's songs helped me so much. God has been so good to me. I meditate to Yolanda's music daily, and her music sets my soul on fire. It makes my heart happy, and I cry and feel the spirit and rejoice in Jesus' name.[2]

As a native Houstonian living in Washington, hope is definitely what keeps me going. No matter where I am, Houston is in my heart and Yolanda's voice is in my CD player.[3]

These are just a few of the examples of what I am talking about. Reading words like these warms my heart. My fans say I help them, but they lift me up too! In the Bible, Proverbs 18:21 says, "The tongue has the power of life and death, and those who love it will eat its fruit" (NIV). When I am choosing songs to sing or writing music I often think of that truth. I make sure my heart is at peace with the message of the words I am singing. There is plenty of music out there today containing words that give negative messages, but I believe I was put on earth to spread the good news of God. I not only want every song I sing to do that, but I want every word I say to do that as well. I've been given a wonderful opportunity to perform all over the world, to speak to people with my radio show, and I am so grateful. But I also know with that comes a great responsibility. Whether I am talking or singing, I choose my words carefully.

Martin Luther King Jr. understood the power of words. Considered among the greatest orators of all time, his "I Have a Dream" speech, delivered on August 28, 1963 from the steps of the Lincoln Memorial is widely considered one of the greatest speeches in history and a pivotal moment for the civil rights movement. The power of Dr. King's words, in that speech and so many others, left an indelible mark on our nation's consciousness. His words predicted a world where people of all races would live together as equals. Many would say that his words paved the way for great change and opportunities for people of color that may not have existed without them.

It's hard to imagine a world where the words of Dr. Martin Luther King Jr. were never heard. I wonder: If he hadn't answered God's call in his life, if he hadn't used his gift and the power of words to inspire change and responsibility, would I be where I am today? Or would the countless doctors, lawyers, and scientists who are people of color be where they are? Would you be able to live where you live? Eat where you eat? Have the friends you have? Attend the school you attend? Would we be able to say the words *President Barack Obama* were it not for the words of Dr. King?

Power Passage

Whatever happens, conduct yourselves in a manner worthy of the gospel of Christ. (Philippians 1:27 NIV)

Point of Practice

Dr. King had a gift for delivering powerful words in his speeches and writings that most of us could only dream of having. Following God's plan and doing God's will were at the core of his life. Volumes have been written about the ugly, hateful words people said against him. Few believed he could have the impact he did on the civil rights movement, as well as the history of our country. Several words from his last speech—"If I can spread the message as the Master taught, then my living will not be in vain"—are evidence that Dr. King knew his purpose in life. He sensed he would die for the words he spoke, but even that didn't stop him from following God's plan for his life. What would the world be like today without the powerful words of Dr. Martin Luther King Jr.?[4]

We too have the ability to move confidently toward the destinies we desire. I was told once by a producer that I should not expect to sell more records than a male singer. I'm so glad that I trusted what God told me and not what that man said. Twenty years, seventeen albums, and $40 million in sales later, I can safely say that there's only one male gospel artist who has sold more albums than I have. He's my little brother in the spiritual sense, Kirk Franklin, whom I love so much!

As children of God, we are never the underdogs. God fully equips us to meet challenges head-on and navigate a future overflowing with His promises for us. Set aside your doubts and trust that He has given you the power to control your destiny; then go out and speak that truth in everything you do. Believe in the bigger and better rather than the here and now.

Second Thessalonians 2:13 says, "We ought always to thank God for you, brothers loved by the Lord, because from the beginning God chose you to be saved through the sanctifying work of the Spirit and through belief in the truth" (NIV). As the Scripture notes, our confidence stems from the fact that we are chosen as God's children. From the beginning He has destined us for great things. Carefully read those powerful words again: "From the beginning God chose you." These words weren't given lightly and shouldn't be taken lightly.

Never believe the misinformation someone tells you or take in negative words about yourself. Your detractors were not present when God revealed His plan to you! Speak the truth about God and spread the good news about the Holy Spirit in everything you say and do. Your words breathe life into your dreams! Your words have power!

Point of Prayer

God, I know as Your child that nothing is impossible. My faith in You is steadfast. In Your words I have the power to be all You want me to be. All I dream for myself is possible with You at my side. I am destined for things greater than I can even imagine: I speak them into the world and so they are.

10 Pensive Points

We have the ability to achieve phenomenal things. The world is ours, as children of God, for the asking. The first step toward our goals is to believe that whatever we dream of is possible: speak it and we can achieve it with God.

1. Take some time today to get quiet. Think back to your childhood. What were your dreams?

2. What did people around you say about those dreams? Did they encourage you?

3. Make two lists, one listing the positive feedback you received about your dreams and one listing the negative feedback. Read over the positive list. Take a red pen and draw a big "X" through the negative list—you won't be needing it!

4. Do some of those dreams still resonate with you? Write them down. Then call someone you trust and tell him or her what you'd like to do.

5. Spend some time daydreaming. Imagine the kind of life you want for yourself today. What does it look like? What would you do for work? Where would you live? How would you dress? Who would your friends be? What does it sound like?

6. Choose at least one thing you could do this week to move yourself closer to your goals. Then tell someone about it.

Ask that person to follow up with you to make sure you've done it.

7. Do you know or admire someone who has the kind of life you'd like to have? Call or write this person, invite him or her out for a cup of tea, and ask questions about how that person achieved his or her goals.

8. Are any obstacles keeping you from the life you want? Are you still hearing those negative words in your mind? What role could your faith play in helping you remove those obstacles? Think about how you could invite God into your process of achieving the kind of life you hope for.

9. Create a visual reminder of one of your dreams. Make a collage using magazine clippings, photos, and other things that will reinforce the possibilities in your mind. Look at it every day as a reminder of your desire to have God's grace in your life.

10. Pay attention to the words you use when talking about your life. Be sure you speak in positive, hopeful ways about your future.

Power Passage

Be very careful, then, how you live—not as unwise but as wise, making the most of every opportunity, because the days are evil. Therefore do not be foolish, but understand what the Lord's will is. (Ephesians 5:15–17 NIV)

I Have Rest and Relaxation in God

I have peace in His presence.

Faith is easy when focus is easy. When our daily routines go unchallenged and our happiness is unfettered, belief in God comes effortlessly. But waters cannot always be still. In the turbulence of life, countless things can upset the boat and instantly transform a calm ride into a bumpy one on chaotic waters.

As you grow and mature in Christ, there's a rest that comes in the comfort of the shelter of God. Rest is the place of decision and meditation. It's the place of joy and assurance. Everyone is given a measure of faith, and it's up to you to rest in your faith.

There's a place in my backyard I retreat to for prayer and reflection. It's a haven from my hustle-and-bustle life. No matter how busy my day is, nothing and no one can take me out of my place of peace because the peace of God is within me. The only way someone can steal it from me is if I give him or her permission. God is our Rock and our Shelter. The Lord will always reward a sincere heart and pure intentions. We can hide in the safety of God.

The Israelites were the great inheritors. They were born blessed with the provision of God and His generous keeping. But the Israelites transformed themselves from great inheritors into great questioners; they paid more heed to their worries than to their blessings. For a people born in faith, they showed very little of it.

Their story of grumbling began in Egypt. Cast under Pharaoh's unforgiving hand, they prayed for deliverance. When God brought them out of slavery through the leadership of Aaron and Moses, they complained about their surroundings, saying that they had left their homes in Egypt to die in a strange and unforgiving desert. They questioned and cried and had no faith in the divine grace of the Lord:

> They quarreled with Moses and said, "If only we had died when our brothers fell dead before the LORD! Why did you bring the LORD's community into this desert, that we and our livestock should die here? Why did you bring us up out of Egypt to this terrible place? It has no grain or figs, grapevines or pomegranates. And there is no water to drink!" (Numbers 20:3–5 NIV)

The Israelites were not satisfied. The Lord offered them peace and provision if they only obeyed in faith, but instead they chose to nurse their worries. As a result, God forced them to "wander in the desert forty years, until the whole generation of those who had done evil in his sight was gone" (Numbers 32:13 NIV). Out of the entire first generation, only Caleb and Joshua were allowed to enter the promised land because they were the only ones who followed the Lord wholeheartedly. The remainder were too fractured and focused on their unhappiness to enter the kingdom divined for God's glory.

Power Passage

The LORD is my shepherd, I shall not be in want.
　　He makes me lie down in green pastures,
he leads me beside quiet waters,
　　he restores my soul. (Psalm 23:1–3 NIV)

Point of Practice

Looking at the Israelites, we sometimes find it hard to imagine they were God's chosen people. Though they were constant recipients of miraculous intervention and divine grace, they grumbled. Verse after verse of the Old Testament relates the chosen ones' great dissatisfaction.

It's easy to stand at a distance and scold the Israelites for their weakling faith, particularly after such extravagant demonstrations of provision and salvation. But we often do the same. We lose sight of the blessings we have; we yearn for what we have yet to possess.

As believers in God, we are called to be faithful and rest in our trust in God. Situations can be complicated, and we might not see how everything will resolve for the good. But God has an impressive record of tying up loose ends and bringing out the best in every circumstance.

What God asked the Israelites to do, and what He continues to ask us to do, is to truly live a life of faith. *Faith*: it's a word we use loosely and often, but it encompasses a large concept. Hebrews 11:1–3 defines the term, saying, "Faith is being sure of what we hope for and certain of what we do not see.... By faith we understand that the universe was formed at God's command, so that what is seen was not made out of what was visible" (NIV).

Faith is not a risk, for we are relying on an infallible God to do the work. When we rely on ourselves and the unpredictable nature of others, our lives are composed of worry, inhibitions, and stress. Faith, however, grants the automatic gift of peace. If we truly allow ourselves to trust in God, we won't ask the questions of how, why, or when. We can understand His timing is perfect and His provision reliable and rest in that knowledge.

Challenge yourself today, tomorrow, and the day after that. As the Israelites proved, faith isn't a choice we make for a period of time; it's a commitment. It's actively choosing again and again to believe in the impossible. When we choose to live that courageous faith, we turn over to God our worry and fear, shed our anxieties. We have the peace and grace of those who truly trust Him.

Point of Prayer

God, I release all worry and claim Your gift of peace. I have faith that once I do all I can do You have it covered, and there is no need for me to worry or stress. I place my trust in You, God, for all my needs, for I know Your understanding and timing are perfect.

10 Pensive Points

In our 24/7 world it is sometimes hard to find time to rest. There is always more we can physically do. It is important to learn to stop and regroup, to let go of the worries and anxieties in life and find a little peace. We can place our trust in the One who already knows everything we need.

1. What is your definition of rest?
2. Do you consider faith a safe or risky concept? How do you show it?
3. List three ways your faith is similar to that of the Israelites.
4. In what area have you recently faltered in your trust in God?

5. What would your state of mind have been in the Israelites' situation if you'd rested in God?

6. Think about times in your life when you have experienced God's blessing only to turn around and feel empty-handed. If you have a journal, write down what your feelings were.

7. Do you believe God is faithful—even to those who consistently doubt?

8. What is one thing in your life that impedes your trusting in God's planned good outcomes for you?

9. What small thing can you do today to lessen that impediment?

10. How does faith in God lead to peace for you?

Power Passage

We know that in all things God works for the good of those who love him, who have been called according to his purpose. (Romans 8:28 NIV)

Chapter Seven

THE POWER OF PRAYER

⚬⚬⚬

"Prayer is not overcoming God's reluctance, but laying hold of His willingness."

—*Martin Luther*

Keeping My Eyes on the Lord Keeps Me from Falling

I am never abandoned.

Communication is key in relating to people. In order for two people to have an effective, fulfilling conversation, each must understand and process the other's statements. So it is with God. Prayer is a conversation with God. It isn't a list of requests from the requester. It is dialogue between God and you. Jesus said to pray believing that God has heard and done something about your concern or request. Then sit calmly to hear the voice of God.

In the song "Be Blessed," I sing about finding a place where you never have to be anything but who you are with God. You don't have to pretend to be something you are not or feel something you don't feel. You can be completely free and honest. You never have to cry or lie. And the Holy Spirit will give you peace through your prayers. When we pray we rest in God's arms; we feel a peace that confirms what our spirits sense. Prayer is a conversation with God that strengthens us and delivers us whenever we need it.

Aron Ralston was only twenty-seven, but he was a veteran climber. He'd trekked up all of Colorado's fourteen-thousand-foot peaks. He'd scaled Mount McKinley. He'd climbed alone in the winter so many times that a day in Utah's Canyonlands National Park seemed routine—so routine that he didn't tell anyone where he was going.

Things went well for the first half of the day. He biked fifteen miles to the Bluejohn Canyon Trailhead and was only 150 yards from the last rappel in the canyon when an eight-hundred-pound boulder, which had seemed secure, started slipping. It shifted and his arm was trapped between the rock and the canyon wall.

Aron's immediate reaction was a rash hope of freeing himself. He tried frantically to move the boulder. He set up ropes and anchors, but nothing worked. He took out his cheap, dulled knife and hacked away at the rock that held him, but it was no use. He was completely stuck. And despite the horror of being trapped, the dangers weren't only in the boulder. It was April, and the temperature fell at night to a harsh thirty degrees. He wore only a T-shirt and shorts and feared hypothermia. He had started the trek with less than a liter of water and found himself in danger of dehydration. Over the next few days, he had to resort to drinking his own urine.

Aron was an optimistic person, but he knew his situation was grave. He'd have to hope for unlikely rescue, sever his arm, or admit that this was where he would die.

On Thursday morning, five days after the accident and as hope was dwindling, Aron saw a picture in his head of the future. He saw a little boy being held by a one-armed man. Caught in the boulder, he knew it was a picture of his son and the life he could have if he could get out.

Aron began to sense a voice, one he described as coming from outside his head but still a part of him. The voice got louder and louder and was shouting at him to use the boulder to break his bones. Eventually, Aron started to pray. He asked for deliverance from the canyon and believes God spoke to him and gave the answer he needed to get himself free. He would have to cut off his arm.

Aron had thought about this before. He had tried on the third day and knew that his blade wasn't sharp enough. It couldn't even cut through the skin. To have any hope, he'd have to break the bones, then carefully and diligently cut through what was left. It would be a painful and dangerous procedure, but it was his only shot at staying alive. On the fifth day, left with no other choices, he broke his bone against the boulder, then proceeded to amputate his arm.

While his action seems an impossibility and a devastation to most, to Aron it was salvation. "The moment when I figured out how I could get free," he said, "it was the best idea and the most beautiful experience I will ever have in my life. . . . It was all euphoria and not a bit of horror. It was having my life back after being dead."[1]

Power Passage

The Lord stood at my side and gave me strength, so that through me the message might be fully proclaimed and all the Gentiles might hear it. And I was delivered from the lion's mouth. The Lord will rescue me from every evil attack and will bring me safely to his heavenly kingdom. To him be glory for ever and ever. Amen. (2 Timothy 4:17–18 NIV)

Point of Practice

Do you remember the childlike wonder with which you embraced everything when you were a kid? You hadn't yet gained your inhibitions, and you approached every situation at full throttle. You weren't afraid to ask questions and believed in things adults had long stopped wishing for, like the ability to fly or be invisible.

God asks you, with a heart as eager as a child's, to step into unbelievable places expecting unbelievable things. He asks us to forsake human frailty for godly faith.

As we get older, faith doesn't come as naturally or as willingly. Like an old boat on the sea, we've been weathered and worn thin by circumstance. Our shell has amassed holes and we're scared to navigate through the dangerous straits. As a result, we look to ourselves to see what we can manage rather than trusting what God can truly manage.

To overcome, God calls us back to our wondrous, childlike faith—a faith we all can conceive again through the power of prayer.

One of my good friends is Dr. Tim Storey. He is known as the "preacher to the stars." He is charismatic, effective, persuasive, and honest. He is an award-winning best-selling author and jewelry designer. We often check on each other as well as pray for one another. One of my favorite Dr. Storey sayings is, "Never lose your innocence." He says that such grown-up things in life as trials, circumstances, losses, and mistakes drain our innocence. We stop laughing, we stop smiling, and we stop taking care of our health. We stop growing…all because we hit one or more bumps on the road of life!

But prayer and relationship with God restores all that. Surround yourself with people who love, support, and appreciate you for you! You need strong prayer warriors who will agree with you as you pursue your purpose. Prayer is pure and powerful. God is not looking for huge, sermonic words of dissertation. He is looking for a simple conversation with His child!

Point of Prayer

God, help me return to a state of childlike wonder toward life. Lord, help me put aside my adult worries and cares and restore me to a place where it is easy to believe all things are possible with You, where I understand life with my heart.

10 Pensive Points

As adults, we sometimes can be too grown up for our own good. We can learn a lot about God's true essence by watching children. Not yet knowing fear or restraint, they live with such abandon. They play with gusto and truly believe they will forever, because life has yet to tell them any different.

1. List situations in your life where you feel you're vulnerable.

2. How does your vulnerability impact your prayer life?

3. Write a prayer in your journal for each vulnerable situation. Visualize how circumstances will turn out if your prayers are answered, if you trust in the Lord rather than in yourself.

4. How has keeping your eyes on the Lord kept you from falling?

5. Think about a few situations where you have felt helpless. How has God intervened?

6. Describe your prayer life.

7. When was the last time you just laughed and played for the fun of it?

8. How can you be more childlike in your faith?

9. Do you call on the Lord every day or only in times of need?

10. What is one small way prayer can help revitalize your faith life?

Power Passage

My eyes are ever on the LORD,
>   for only he will release my feet from the snare.
>   (Psalm 25:15 NIV)

Nothing Is Impossible for God; Therefore, Nothing Is Impossible for Me

I ask and I shall receive.

I am a believer and I worship an all-knowing, all-powerful God—a God who parted seas, performed miracles, healed the sick, and raised the dead. Regardless of our denominations or affiliations, we all believe there is nothing beyond the Lord's power. And yet while we claim to believe in a God who dispenses the impossible for others every day, we often hesitate to believe God will do the same for us. I used to ask myself, *How?* Some things just seem too impossible.

Before the foundation of the world, God mapped out my life. The Lord sees far beyond my finite vision. The Holy Spirit knows beyond my limited intelligence, and I believe I'm pretty smart! I've learned to trust God far beyond what I see and feel, which always broadens my faith! Consider this: if we falter, perhaps it isn't our God who is small, but our vision. God is a big God. The Lord is waiting to help you achieve big things. If you want to be successful in your life, you have to have a big vision. Without a big vision you can't have big dreams. Think big for your life.

Chris Gardner learned how to think big. If you looked at his life statistically, his chances at success were small. Born into a broken home with weak morals, Chris Gardner endured childhood as a kid who was physically and sexually abused. His mother, despite being a woman endowed with heart and confidence, spent time in jail for welfare fraud and kept a boyfriend who brought little to their lives but beatings. She passed on her love and encouragement but could offer little more. Chris spent his youth slipping in and out of foster care. He had intellect and potential, but little hope.

At eighteen, Chris joined the U.S. Navy. There he started training to become a medic, a position that, he thought, would pull him out of poverty. But that dream changed when he met a man in a red Ferrari who earned $80,000 a month. The man was a stockbroker. From there, his vision took on a new face.

When his son, Chris Gardner Jr., was born in 1981, more changed than family dynamics. Committed to living the dreams etched in his head and heart, Chris gave up his medical sales job for a position he was lucky to land in a broker-training program. But when his hiring manager was fired the position fell through. Chris, a man with a new son, was left with no job and no income. Misfortune multiplied when he was thrown in jail for unpaid parking tickets, and his girlfriend left him with sole responsibility for his two-year-old son.

Chris had no experience, no diploma, and no contacts, but he had the gift of persistence. After getting out of jail, he earned a spot in another stock brokerage training program. It offered a stipend too meager to pay for both his son's day care and an apartment. With few options, he made the only choice he could: he started his apprenticeship at one of the nation's foremost brokerage firms as a homeless man.

For a year, as Chris trained, he lived on the streets with his son. They found beds in San Francisco's overcrowded homeless shelters. They created living quarters out of street corners. They passed many cold nights in the four walls of BART station's public bathrooms. Chris worked hard. His work ethic rivaled that of others who were vying for top slots in the competitive field. He became the best among his colleagues. He never breathed a word to anyone that he was homeless.

After passing the training program, Chris caught the attention of a prominent employer who offered Chris a position. After more than a year of struggle and heartache, he finally had money to get off the streets, into reliable housing, and find a good day care for his son.

Chris wasn't satisfied. He learned more, impressed more, and climbed the ladder with the tenacity of a man still fighting the streets.

He was transferred to the company's New York office and then decided to do the impossible: launch his own firm. With start-up capital of a mere $10,000, a small apartment, and a solitary wooden desk that served as both office space and a dinner table, Chris once again made his risk pay off. He became a multimillionaire and philanthropist. His work, not surprisingly, focused on helping the homeless. "I didn't know that you couldn't do it," he said. "So I did it."[1]

Power Passage

With man this is impossible, but with God all things are possible. (Matthew 19:26 NIV)

Point of Practice

Chris Gardner is a revolutionary. "My first ambition in life was to be Miles Davis," he said. "I studied trumpet for ten years. I didn't want to be a jazz artist. I wanted to be Miles Davis. My mom sat me down and said, 'You can't be Miles Davis. He already has that job. You have to be Chris.' That freaked me out. I mean, who is Chris? All I knew is I wanted to be world-class at something."[2]

One of my favorite things about Chris's story is that he said, "I didn't know that you couldn't do it, so I did it!" That has been a part of my life experience. I told a reporter for the Gospel Music Channel that there's a confidence with which I approach every task. If God put it in my hands, I'm obligated to do it. Never think you can't do something; just know you have to get it done! I've never thought I would fail at anything I loved to do! The only person who can put a ceiling on your potential is you. Never accept anyone's limitations or boxes for your life.

Luke 18:27 confirms the truth: "What is impossible with men is possible with God" (NIV).

Challenge your glass ceilings every day. Remove the preexisting limitations set on your dreams and ask God the big question.

Point of Prayer

God, I ask You to help me pursue the deepest dreams of my heart. I look past any limitations and see only possibilities for myself. I know that with You at my side I can achieve anything. With You, Lord, I dream big. I ask, and it will be given to me.

10 Pensive Points

Often the only limits we truly have in life are the ones we place on ourselves. Spend some time thinking about things you would like to do in your life. Dream big. Then set out to cocreate your life with the Lord. With God at your side, nothing is impossible.

1. What do you believe is impossible?
2. Now define what *impossible* means to God.

3. In your journal, list your glass ceilings.

4. List fears that play into the pursuit of your dreams.

5. Across from each item on your lists, note one thing you can do to challenge it. Think "off the board" and if you need help, ask a trusted friend to think with you.

6. Now, on the same list, note how going to the Lord in prayer can help eliminate those struggles.

7. If you were given the ability to do *anything*, what one thing would it be?

8. What have you seen occur recently that you believed was impossible?

9. Stop right now and pray. Ask God for wisdom to reveal your heart's deepest desires and the steps you should take to pursue them. Take a risk and believe in return He will take a risk on you.

10. Note your prayer in your journal with today's date.

Power Passage

Ask and it will be given to you; seek and you will find; knock and the door will be opened to you. (Matthew 7:7 NIV)

Intercession Assures Answered Prayer

God is the Great Answerer.

I was blessed to be born into a very loving, close-knit family. We were raised to believe we could do anything we set our minds to. Growing up, we did everything together. We pushed one another creatively. We laughed, cried, and played together. We ran, swam, and worked out together. Of all the things we did together—and continue to do!—the most important was pray. Today, we all still call and ask other family members to agree in prayer as we move in purpose!

The beauty of prayer is that God always answers. I've written and sung many songs about prayer because it's such an important part of my relationship with God. God is always just a prayer away.

Always approach God with eager expectation. God finds pleasure in answering your pure prayer, your heartfelt plea on behalf of another, your request of His great hand of mercy. Faithfully commit yourself to the art of asking. It will open doors to answered prayers in ways you never could have imagined. Faithful petitioners are faithfully answered.

Abraham is one of the most faithful servants of God in the Bible, one of God's greatest followers. The strength of Abraham's faith was his *relationship* with God. Abraham spoke with the Lord as he would a friend. He was respectful, certainly, but he was also honest, concerned, vulnerable, and forthright. Abraham grew strong in his faith and understanding because he was willing to petition the Lord.

In the book of Genesis, the Cities of the Plain play a prominent role. When Abraham and his nephew Lot decided to part, Abraham went the way of Canaan, and Lot chose the plain, near Sodom and on the Jordan River, an area excellent for herding cattle and producing food but also famously rife with sin. The inhabitants of the cities of Sodom and Gomorrah were, as written in the book of Ezekiel, "arrogant, overfed and unconcerned; they did not help the poor and needy. They were haughty and did detestable things" (16:49–50 NIV). Abraham was well aware of their deplorable ways, yet he had a heart for the region because his family lived there.

The Bible says that the sins of the cities grew so severe that God settled on destroying them. But before the Lord did that, God approached Abraham and let him know of His plan. "The outcry against Sodom and Gomorrah is so great and their sin so grievous that I will go down and see if what they have done is as bad as the outcry that has reached me" (Genesis 18:20–21 NIV).

Though Abraham understood the extent of the sin in the area, he remembered his family and desperately bargained for their safekeeping. Instead of simply agreeing with the Lord's decision, Abraham said, "Will you sweep away the righteous with the wicked? What if there are fifty righteous people in the city?" (Genesis 18:23–24 NIV).

Instead of being angered by Abraham's response, God listened. He promised Abraham if there were fifty righteous men in the city, God would spare it. But Abraham was not content with such a response and persisted. *And what about forty-five? Forty? Thirty? Twenty?* He continued until he reached the low sum of ten righteous individuals, and the Lord again promised mercy on the whole city, saying, "For the sake of ten, I will not destroy it" (Genesis 18:32 NIV). With this, Abraham was content and could not dispute the justice of the Lord.

Sodom was still destroyed. The sin was so prevalent and the righteous so few, the city could not be spared. The city burned in sulfur thrown from the heavens, and all the evil within was shattered. And while the city had to be destroyed, God still wanted to honor Abraham's intercession. The Lord sent angels warning Abraham's nephew Lot of the impending doom and helped him escape. The Lord respected Abraham's plea while maintaining righteous judgment. God's mercy was due to Abraham's intercession.

Power Passage

I know that the LORD saves his anointed;
    he answers him from his holy heaven
    with the saving power of his right hand.
Some trust in chariots and some in horses,
    but we trust in the name of the LORD our God.
They are brought to their knees and fall,
    but we rise up and stand firm.
    (Psalm 20:6–8 NIV)

Point of Practice

The Bible is full of acts of intercession, people who filled in the gap between individuals and God. Their cries convey everything from needs of mercy to justice, salvation, and safekeeping. While Abraham's petition for grace on behalf of Sodom is among the most marked acts of intercession, prayers of pleading dot the Old and New Testaments. Isaiah prayed for the safekeeping of a nation. Stephen prayed for the mercy of those who would murder him, his last words being, "Lord, do not hold this sin against them" (Acts 7:60 NIV). Nehemiah prayed diligently about the rebuilding of Jerusalem. Time after time, Christ's followers asked Him about what was important to them, and the Lord was willing to respond.

Intercessory prayer continues in our present day. Just as God listened to Abraham, Moses, and the apostles and disciples of Jesus Christ, the Lord opens His ears to you. The Holy Spirit respects and appreciates your genuine appeals for those you care about and will respond accordingly.

Intercession is prayer on behalf of someone else as though the burden is our own. Pray for your family, your pastor, your government, and your president. Your intercession may be the lifeline they need.

Point of Prayer

God, You always answer my prayers for myself, but today I am requesting Your help and guidance for others. Please bless my friends and family, clergy, coworkers, and others I come into contact with on a daily basis and help them know Your mercy and grace as I do. Protect and keep them safe as You keep me. Lead them to Your perfect plan in their lives as You lead me to mine.

10 Pensive Points

Prayer is powerful. It is not only to be used for ourselves, but as believers we can call upon the Lord on behalf of the people in our lives we love and care about. The span of God's love is so powerful its reach is far and wide.

1. In your journal, define *intercession* in your own words.

2. Think of two ways intercession can be a more powerful tool in your faith.

3. Search your Bible and discover another instance where intercession was used.

4. Consider why dialoguing with God is important.

5. Do you believe God will always respond?

6. List ways God has responded to you in the past.

7. What is one way you can use the power of prayer in your life today?

8. List instances in which you have interceded for others and how those situations turned out.

9. List one hindrance you face in giving your requests to God.

10. Ask a trusted friend to help you brainstorm five ways to address that hindrance.

Power Passage

We say with confidence,
"The Lord is my helper; I will not be afraid.
What can man do to me?" (Hebrews 13:6 NIV)

Chapter Eight

THE POWER OF PEACE

"Peace is not merely a distant goal that we seek
but a means by which we arrive at that goal."

—*Martin Luther King Jr.*

Inner Peace Builds
Outer Strength

My core is my heart.

My family says I'm one of the calmest people they know. I rarely frown or become frustrated under pressure. Even though I regularly perform in front of thousands of people, I am introverted. When it comes to showing my emotions, it's not until someone has pushed me far beyond the limit of tolerance that I raise an eyebrow or voice my displeasure.

God has given us the power of peace. The message in the song "That Name" is an important one. Just saying God's name can calm our souls and relieve our fears. Just speaking the name of Jesus, aloud or in silent prayer, can give us the peace we seek. Whenever I call on the Lord's name, I immediately begin to feel lighter. I know that no matter what I am dealing with, I am not alone.

You can tap into the peace Isaiah talks about in the Scriptures (Isaiah 26:3–4) if you rely on the totality and constant nature of God: "You will keep in perfect peace him whose mind is steadfast, because he trusts in you" (verse 3 NIV).

God is all and in all. That is His omnipotence. All-powerful, almighty, all–wondrous—these are merely finite human descriptions, and yet we know Him to always remain faithful.

God desires trust from and fulfillment for each of us. He wants us to shed our unrest and open our eyes to His grand tranquillity. When we do this, we experience an anointed peace that withstands any pressure, pain, or trial.

In the 2008 Beijing Olympics, Michael Phelps won eight gold medals, bringing his lifetime collection to a hefty fourteen. While his success in the water brought him worldwide attention and public acclaim, the tide of public opinion turned on him almost as quickly when in early 2009 pictures surfaced of Michael smoking marijuana. Phelps was attacked in the press for his behavior, accused of being a poor role model, suspended by USA Swimming from competitive swimming for three months, and lost major endorsement deals. However, this was not the first time Phelps had to triumph over what at first appeared to be an impossible burden.

He was born at an impressive nine pounds, six ounces, and was twenty-three inches long. He's maintained the awe-inducing size. At six foot four and 195 pounds, he's walking muscle. Yet the biggest noticeable difference isn't his bulk, but his proportion. Phelps's "wingspan" is an incredible three inches longer than his height. His torso matches that of a man four inches taller, which also increases his reach. And all that weight and length funnel down to a slim thirty-two-inch waist. And while the sturdy top half is impressive and pushes him through the water with uncommon speed and force, it isn't enough. Phelps's legs are about four inches shorter than average, which inevitably helps with treading in the water, and with size fourteen feet, he's been blessed with built-in flippers. He has the ideal body for a swimmer.

His distinctive size and shape have worked to his benefit in the pool, but they weren't always characteristics that made him happy. "He loved swimming from a very young age," said his mother, Debbie Phelps. "And it helped build his self-esteem and his confidence. But as Michael reached more advanced levels of training, he was put with older kids who often bullied him. He could sometimes be a little 'twit' because he wanted attention, but he was also teased about things he had no control over. His wingspan was wider than his height, so when he was an adolescent, his hands were down around his knees, and he had big ears."

Michael's unlikely size wasn't his only issue. He suffered from attention deficit/hyperactivity disorder (ADHD). He had trouble sitting still and concentrating. He was overly active, so much so that one of his teachers told his mother, "Your son will never be able to focus on anything."

Michael's mom took him to the doctor and he was put on Ritalin at the age of nine. After two years on meds, he wanted to find a different way to be able to focus and keep still. He found that grounding in swimming. By age twelve, swimming was his life, and he was practicing for an hour and a half in the morning before school and nearly three hours after. By fifteen, he had attended his first Olympics. By sixteen, he was setting world records and by nineteen he was back in the Olympic pool, only this time lapping up medals. By twenty-three, he was an international sensation, earning eight gold medals in Beijing.

At the end of his three-month suspension, Michael Phelps returned to the pool. He released a statement saying, "I engaged in behavior which was regrettable and demonstrated bad judgment. I'm 23 years old and despite the successes I've had in the pool, I acted in a youthful and inappropriate way, not in a manner people have come to expect from me. For this, I am sorry. I promise my fans and the public it will not happen again."

Whether or not Michael Phelps will triumph over his most recent obstacle remains to be seen, but his willingness to take responsibility for his behavior, admit his mistake, and get back to the work of honoring his God-given gift of swimming is certainly a good start and exactly what God expects of all of us.[1]

Power Passage

He must seek peace and pursue it. (1 Peter 3:11 NIV)

Point of Practice

Have you ever said, "I bet no one in the world is going through what I am going through"? Every time you say this, pinch yourself and say, "Not true!" So many famous professional, successful people we know have had to overcome some hurdle for their greatness to break forth. Tom Cruise has dyslexia; Halle Berry is deaf in one ear; Nick Jonas has diabetes. But these issues did not deter them from pursuing their passions and dreams. ADHD could not stop Michael Phelps. It actually kept him excited about swimming. He found peace in the pool.

Often our blessings come in disguise. Those out-of-the-ordinary things about us can make us uncomfortable, but they are also what make us special.

Consider your life. What traits are out of the ordinary, what desires are different—what sets you apart? Instead of seeing your differences as negatives, see them as potential blessings. You have ability no one else has. Genesis 1:27 says, "God created man in his own image, in the image of God he created him; male and female he created them" (NIV). Those simple words are powerful reminders that you are God-breathed. Every part of you, even those differences, is from the hand of God.

Point of Prayer

God, it is easy to see the good parts of my life as a blessing. But Lord, please help me see all of my life as God-breathed, even the challenges. I know all is delivered by Your hand. Help me grow and stretch into an example of Your love in the world.

10 Pensive Points

We all are children of God. Each of us is created in His vision with unique qualities, likes and dislikes, talents and skills. God loves us as we are. Rather than wishing you were someone or something different, embrace who you are, celebrate yourself as God does, and see how your life changes for the better.

1. What is "inner peace" to you?
2. Take a walk, a swim, a long bath, or perform whatever activity gives you peace. Take along a notepad and list the obstacles you have to overcome to make this activity a regular part of your life.
3. Consider how inner peace can play a role in your success.
4. How does confidence instigate peace?
5. What prevents you from being at peace with yourself?
6. Begin to see your differences as strengths by listing a positive benefit you have experienced because of each one. Ask a trusted friend for help with this if you need it.
7. Ask God how you can use these differences to His glory.
8. Focus on one other person you can help become comfortable with his or her own special characteristics.

9. Write a prayer on your calendar asking God to help you move toward inner peace to build outer strength.

10. Select a prayer partner and pray the Point of Prayer together daily for forty days.

Power Passage

I know that there is nothing better for men than to be happy and do good while they live. That everyone may eat and drink, and find satisfaction in his toil—this is the gift of God. (Ecclesiastes 3:12–13 NIV)

God, the Great Peacemaker, Can Still Any Storm

I place my faith in the God who knows the outcome of every circumstance.

We have all been in situations we thought would be the end of us. Relationships, financial crises, emotional battles can all press us to the point where we ask ourselves, *When will this end?* Whenever such things overwhelm you, rely on the words of Luke: "Nothing is impossible with God" (Luke 1:37 NIV).

That day wasn't supposed to be about her. It was July 2007, and Robin Roberts had just finished working on a tribute to her former colleague, Joel Siegel, who had died the previous month of colon cancer. She got home late that night, incredibly tired, and was getting ready for bed when she felt a lump in her right breast. She was startled, but, like most women would do, she tried to convince herself it was nothing.

The next day, though, Robin went to the doctor. It was a precautionary measure, she told herself. Just a checkup. Despite her hope that she was unnecessarily worried, something was there. The mammogram missed it, but the ultrasound picked it up. The doctor called her on the phone, catching her as she was getting off a plane. His words were simple: "Robin, it's cancer."

"I remember being angry at my body because it had betrayed me for the first time," she said. "I felt embarrassed because I've always spouted off about how I eat right, stay active, don't smoke, and take care of myself. Yet here I was with cancer." After considering whether or not to keep the cancer private, Robin decided to go on the air and talk about it. Her mother had always told her to "make her mess her message," and Robin had always considered her audience her "extended family." Despite the difficulty of admitting such a personal matter on such a public platform, she knew she could encourage and inspire others who were enduring the same heartache. She could educate millions on the need for early detection and the ability to be a survivor.

The calls rolled in. People from all over wanted to share their messages of thanks, encouragement, and consolation. It was an outpouring of love from strangers and survivors.

Robin was raised on faith. In Robin's close-knit family, church and God were important parts of life. As a child if she was too sick to go to church, she was too sick to go out and play for the rest of the weekend. Spirituality continues to play a vital role in Robin's life as an adult; she says her relationship with God is a comfort and a bond she shares with her family members. Phone calls with her sister always end in prayer, even when she is talking from her office.

Robin's mother taught her the "prayer of protection" when she first moved away from home. She has said it every morning for the last twenty years before going out the door: "The light of God surrounds me. The love of God enfolds me. The power of God protects me. The presence of God watches over me. Wherever I am, God is."

Robin's surgery was successful and the cancer was contained, but there was bad news too: she was going to need chemotherapy.

For cancer patients, chemotherapy can be a devastating experience. It means weeks of losing energy and losing hair.

Robin had eight treatments. By the second, her hair began falling out. While she at first wore wigs on the air to cover up the hair loss, she decided her hair loss was a part of her story too. Her hair loss was another way to show people that they could get through cancer and be okay. She decided to take off her wig. She was going to bare it all.

Robin took another large step during New York City's Fashion Week. She had made pacts with her coworkers to pursue challenges and found herself a model during the week, walking the runway in an Isaac Mizrahi dress. She took to the runway as a cancer patient—wigless. In front of a massive crowd, she redefined beauty.

Robin believes an inner life is crucial to true success and that her faith sustains her. It clearly helped her cope with her illness. She says she asks for God's grace every morning, and just for that day. She doesn't worry about anything but the present. And the next day, she starts the morning in the same way, asking for God's grace again.[1]

Power Passage

Peace I leave with you; my peace I give you. I do not give to you as the world gives. Do not let your hearts be troubled and do not be afraid. (John 14:27 NIV)

Point of Practice

I was in Tennessee when I heard Robin was battling cancer. I started praying for her because I can imagine the pain and anguish that come with such a diagnosis. As I walked through the Grand Ole Opry Hotel, a beautiful woman stopped me. She introduced herself as Robin's mom. I hugged her and told her I'd been praying for Robin. Tears filled her eyes as she said, "So many people love my Robin."

In times of distress and pressure we find out how many people truly love us!

We are human and we hurt. God never said that we would have beds of roses and lives of ease once we recognized Him as King and Lord. In fact, the truth is quite to the contrary. Jesus said, "In this world you will have trouble. But take heart! I have overcome the world" (John 16:33 NIV).

As with Robin Roberts, our storms don't have to beat us. When we're able to take our eyes off what is hurting us and focus on what heals us, we are given the power to beat the unbeatable.

As Christians, we believe our solution is in the power of God. The elements around us are often too big for us to handle on our own. There are things we can't control and outcomes we can't predict. But nothing is too big for God to handle.

Point of Prayer

The light of God surrounds me. The love of God enfolds me. The power of God protects me. The presence of God watches over me. Wherever I am, God is.

10 Pensive Points

Prayer is powerful. We can confidently call on God at any time through prayer and connect with the Lord from wherever we are. Prayer brings the Lord front and center into our lives and makes God real. Consistent prayer can open our world in ways we never imagined.

1. Think about the state of your prayer life. Is it active? Nonexistent?

2. What were some of your favorite prayers as a child?

3. Do you tend to pray to God when things are good? Or do you pray only when you have challenges?

4. Have you ever known someone with a serious illness? What role did prayer play in that person's recovery?

5. For the next week, set aside two minutes each morning to pray.

6. At the end of the week, take some time to write in your journal about any changes you've noticed during the week.

7. When you pray, how do you talk to God? Do you worry about what to say?

8. Do you think there is a right way to pray?

9. Try thinking of praying like having a conversation with your best friend.

10. At the end of the day, write down the ways your prayers have been answered. Remember to say, "Thank You."

Power Passage

Is any one of you in trouble? He should pray. Is anyone happy? Let him sing songs of praise. Is any one of you sick? He should call the elders of the church to pray over him and anoint him with oil in the name of the Lord. And the prayer offered in faith will make the sick person well; the Lord will raise him up. If he has sinned, he will be forgiven. Therefore confess your sins to each other and pray for each other so that you may be healed. The prayer of a righteous man is powerful and effective. (James 5:13–16 NIV)

God Will Grant Me Rest When I Guard My Heart

I protect the most valuable part of myself.

When the Bible refers to the heart, it means the emotions. God created us with hearts to love. We can love purely and simply. We can withstand the harshest, most severe crises and love even harder. Despite this strength, the heart—our emotional center—is quite fragile. It can be easily broken. As followers of Christ, we must protect our hearts, for it is with the heart we believe. When God has not given you peace in your heart about something, be very cautious about pursuing, believing, or doing it.

I write and sing from my heart. And that's why I think so many of my fans comment that they can relate to my music—we all have hearts. I even once had a man who called himself an atheist say he converted to Christianity because he realized that one of my songs could have come only through God—only God could produce a song so powerful. People love my music because they can hear my heart in it. It makes them think, *Wow, Yolanda's been through the same thing I have; she made it, and I can make it through too.*

One of the greatest betrayals in the stories of the Bible resulted in the greatest act of salvation; it is the story of Judas's treachery. Throughout the New Testament, we witness Jesus interacting with His disciples, growing a ministry of amazing power. We hear very little about one of the key characters in the gospel: Judas. It isn't until the end that we get a closer picture of the man who gave Jesus up to those who would condemn Him to death.

As we all know, the scene unfolds at dinner. Jesus and His twelve disciples are around the table. It's the Last Supper and over the meal, Jesus makes an incredible accusation: "I tell you the truth, one of you will betray me" (Matthew 26:21 NIV).

Faces fill with shock. The table is full of Jesus' most trusted and loved. That one of them would betray Him seems unthinkable. One by one, they adamantly deny it, going around the table professing their innocence by saying, "Surely not I, Lord?" (26:22 NIV). And one by one, Jesus absolves them—all of them except Judas.

Like the others, Judas says, "Surely not I, Rabbi?" (26:25 NIV). But this time Jesus answers, "Yes, it is you" (26:25 NIV).

Jesus' accusation was true. Earlier, Judas had approached the chief priests and asked, "What are you willing to give me if I hand him over to you?" (26:15 NIV). They counted out thirty silver coins. After the monetary transaction, Judas bided his time, waiting for an opportunity to hand Jesus over to the authorities.

The chance Judas was looking for came at Gethsemane. Judas arrived with a crowd as Jesus was speaking, and he kissed Him on the face, saying, "Greetings, Rabbi!" (26:49 NIV). His sign of friendship was also his sign of betrayal, and Jesus was immediately arrested.

After taking Jesus away, the chief priests and elders gathered to determine what Jesus' punishment would be. They decided on the death sentence. While Judas could endure handing Jesus over, the death sentence woke him up to his actions. Guilt plagued him. He was filled with deep regret and took his thirty coins back to the men who paid him, saying, "I have sinned, for I have betrayed innocent blood" (27:4 NIV). But even they, the morally corrupt, would not pocket the money for they considered it blood money. So Judas left and, unable to endure his own conscience, hanged himself.

Power Passage

Teach me your way, O LORD,
     and I will walk in your truth;
give me an undivided heart,
     that I may fear your name. (Psalm 86:11 NIV)

Point of Practice

As the story of Judas's great betrayal has been read and reread, it is easy for us to lift our noses in disgust. *Who,* we think, *could possibly betray Jesus? Who would want to?* But the truth is, Judas stands as a symbol of the potential within us all to think of ourselves over others, to forsake our morals and principles for material gain.

During Jesus' arrest and crucifixion, none of the twelve disciples were rooted boldly in faith or standing beside Jesus. Instead, they hid meekly and watched as Christ suffered alone. Peter denied Jesus three times. It was Jesus' closest and most trusted companions who forsook Him.

God tells us to guard our hearts above all else because He's incredibly aware of the human inclination to grow weak and give in. He knows that even the best of us have a potential to inflict great pain. He knows that those closest to us can hurt us the most.

Guarding our hearts *doesn't* mean not trusting God. It means protecting ourselves from ideas and beliefs that could hurt us. The best way to guard your heart is not to be a recluse, but instead to be a connoisseur of the Word of God. Pad your inner walls with the truth of the salvation you have in Christ. Understand His deeper love and stay rooted in His principles.

It's impossible for us to walk through life without pain. We will be hurt, certainly. We will feel betrayed. God shows us that when we protect our hearts, we can respond in strength instead of weakness. As Jesus did, we can show mercy instead of hate.

Jesus' words on the cross were not words of damnation, self-pity, or anger; they were words of selfless wisdom: "Father, forgive them," He said, "for they do not know what they are doing" (Luke 23:34 NIV).

His words were the ultimate display of strength in the ultimate moment of pain. He showed us a lesson we can believe in now: our hearts can be strong even when everything else is breaking. Our hearts truly are the wellspring of life.

Point of Prayer

God, I know in You my heart is protected. People may disappoint me, but I know that You never will. Help me be like Jesus. Even when my heart is broken, I ask You to help me be forgiving and strong, like Him.

10 Pensive Points

It is sometimes hard not to act on our emotions. When our hearts are hurting we want to seek revenge, thinking it will relieve us of our pain. How can you guard your heart in God and respond to hurt more as Jesus did?

1. How do you normally express emotion?
2. Have you ever had a Judas in your life? How did you handle it?

3. If you lashed out at the person who hurt you, how did you feel afterward?

4. Write down some ways you could have handled the situation differently, after reading the story of Jesus and Judas.

5. What role does forgiveness play in your life?

6. Are you quick to forgive, or do you hold grudges? How does this affect your relationships?

7. Have you ever been a Judas?

8. How did it make you feel?

9. List some ways you can make amends after you have hurt someone.

10. How could a guarded heart bring you peace?

Power Passage

Wisdom will enter your heart, and knowledge will be pleasant to your soul. (Proverbs 2:10 NIV)

I Need Not Worry—God Is in Control

I am in the hands of a higher power.

I don't really worry about much! Worrying is a waste of time. The energy I spend worrying could be used to pray for answers to the questions about my dilemma.

Let me define *worry*. Worry to me is overly intense concern about a situation or a person. It's perfectly fine to be concerned. But when your concern turns into fear, anxiety, hopelessness, and depression, it has developed into worry. God has given provisions for worry in Scripture. He created His peace for these times. You cannot live life without distraction or discomfort. They are realities. God, however, knows the outcome. He sees the miracle beyond today. He sees the answers and solutions because He *is* the answer and the solution.

We are so awesomely created. My prayer is to help you train your mind to understand the power God has placed inside you. What I am about to say is a concept so profound you might miss it: *You can conquer worry by not worrying!* It is a principle from ages of experience and wisdom.

God has shown me clearly that He was in control in so many instances. No matter how much I cried, yelled, or screamed, nothing changed until I rested in His peace.

God's presence brings you another level of calm. But you must be willing to go into His sheltering, loving arms!

One Christmas season, things were really tough. As the oldest of the family, I have always felt a sense of responsibility when it comes to providing for and protecting my siblings. Throughout the year, I helped everyone weather storms and bumps. It was December, and I was wondering how in the world I was going to pull off this Christmas celebration.

I looked in the pantry and said, "Lord, I need Your help!" Growing up in church, I have heard "mailbox testimonies" time and time again. Those are stories of unexpected financial miracles that come in the mail. From Reverend Ike to Reverend Oral Roberts, it seemed everyone had experienced a mailbox miracle. I hadn't.

It was after 8:00 p.m. and God told me to go to the mailbox. Can you imagine going to the mailbox on a cold December night because you thought you heard God tell you to? Well, the voice was so strong that I went out to the front yard without a coat to retrieve the mail. It was dark, and I couldn't see what I had. When I got back inside I flipped through the letters. I had circulars, periodicals, and a check from my writing company!

Now when things get a little shaky and uncertain, I have a new perspective. My first reaction is to pray, "God, You are in control. Nothing takes You by surprise. I believe You have a way that I must take, and I expect a blessing concerning this. I will stay in Your presence and rely on Your peace that passes understanding. Amen!"

When worry sets in, don't panic! Stay calm and start praying! God has never and will never take you through anything you are incapable of overcoming while you're in the Lord's hands!

Power Passage

Do not worry about your life, what you will eat or drink; or about your body, what you will wear. Is not life more important than food, and the body more important than clothes? Look at the birds of the air; they do not sow or reap or store away in barns, and yet your heavenly Father feeds them. Are you not much more valuable than they? Who of you by worrying can add a single hour to his life? (Matthew 6:25–27 NIV)

Point of Practice

God calls us not to worry, but we often misinterpret His message. He isn't asking us to forget or be complacent about our issues. God wants us to understand our role and His role. In Matthew 6:25–27, God confirms what we already know: He is looking out for us. He knows the number of hairs on our heads, what we eat, who our parents are, where we live—every little thing. When we get caught up in our own worry, we forget we worship an incredibly aware God. He knows our situation backward and forward. He knows what we need and desire and, as always, will provide for us in His abundance and in His due timing.

When we're able to understand this greater provision, our worry lessens. Our nervous nature shifts to confidence in knowing we are taken care of.

When you sense worry sneaking up on you, set aside time to pray. Tell Him about what's troubling you and what your heart hopes for. God lifts our burdens in numerous ways. While some circumstances will take patience and trust, other times God will open doors for us that we can walk through. Not worrying doesn't mean we can't be active pursuers of full and healthy lives. Practice patience, look for His solutions, and embrace the opportunities that come to your door.

Point of Prayer

God, I know You are always right on time. Help me stay faithful to You and continue to pursue an active, healthy, full life even when things start to look shaky. Help me have patience and trust that You have every situation in Your sights and that You have already set my path. All I have to do is walk it.

10 Pensive Points

God always knows exactly what we need and when we need it. The Lord may not show up exactly when we think He should. Yet the Holy Spirit's timing is always perfect.

1. Collect as many "mailbox testimonies" as you can. If possible, get one each day for the next month.

2. Journal your own mailbox miracle.

3. List your three biggest worries.

4. Write yourself the imaginary letter, check, official document, whatever would be the mailbox miracle to cross off one of the items on your worry list.

5. Read it to those around you whose lives are affected by the worry item.

6. Use the imaginary letter as the basis for prayer.

7. For each item on your worry list, pray for faith that will remove your worry.

8. What is one thing you can do to show you believe God is really in control?

9. What is one fun, simple thing you enjoy that combats stress in your life?

10. Mark on your calendar a date and time to do it.

Power Passage

The Lord gives strength to his people;
    the Lord blesses his people with peace.
    (Psalm 29:11 NIV)

Chapter Nine

THE POWER OF PROTECTION

⁙

"When I am afraid, I will trust in you."

—*Psalm 56:3 NIV*

"He who dwells in the shelter of the Most High
will rest in the shadow of the Almighty.
I will say of the LORD, 'He is my refuge and my fortress,
my God, in whom I trust.' "

—*Psalm 91:1–2 NIV*

God Is Ever Watchful and Responsive

He is my constant protector.

Our vision is never total. Our eyesight is limited. We're near-sighted. We're farsighted. Our peripheral vision can be poor, and sometimes the fog rolls in so heavy that we can't see more than five feet in front of us. It's hard to know if we're headed in the right direction. God has divine vision. He is the great Overseer who knows our every step and every destination. He is with us every step of the way, guiding us to safety.

I started thinking about the countless times God's hand of protection has been around me. He keeps, protects, and comforts my daughter, Taylor, and me. I don't have to navigate through doubt and uncertainty because God has lovingly paved the way.

Pastor Bill Winston reminded me that my destiny is in my hands. No one else has anything to do with my potential, my purpose, or the propensity of where and how far I can go.

God even protects us from ourselves. There are times when a romance ends just before the wedding because God sees a detrimental outcome. Sometimes a promotion is not received because the person could become complacent as a result. We are created for motion! We are to be about the Father's business. No admirable character in the Bible sat on the porch all day waiting for a move of God! We are to be mobile in our careers, in our families, and in our fitness.

There is no such thing as a couch potato ministry. Jesus said, "Go"! Go into the world and preach, teach, and baptize. Stay fresh and don't get stale. Stagnant things putrefy after a while. Stay active in the Spirit.

I travel a lot. I love singing and touring because I get a chance to see the people I have affected and influenced. I have to travel on a tour bus if we're doing lots of cities within a short amount of time. These buses are huge and carry ten to sixteen people very comfortably. We have front and back lounges and condo bunks for sleeping.

I remember one winter the roads were very icy and snow had fallen for several weeks. I was a bit concerned for our safety. Instead of worrying, I prayed. God then gave me a peace that everything would be fine.

Early one morning, at about 3:00 a.m., I felt the bus swerving a little. I reminded God of His promise to me and everyone on that bus, including Taylor, who never woke up. In a matter of seconds the bus was straight and moving forward.

The bus driver told us later that a car had been in the road and he had maneuvered to miss it. He said it could have been fatal, but God was with us. Hallelujah! The protection of God is real! Trust God for the protection of your family, your friends, your business, and your life. He never fails!

Power Passage

You are my hiding place;
> you will protect me from trouble
> and surround me with songs of deliverance.
> (Psalm 32:7 NIV)

Point of Practice

God is all-powerful: I repeat these words when I encounter a situation that seems beyond my physical strength to handle. One of my dearest friends always tells me that everything we encounter or attempt to overcome is a matter of perspective. He says that if we look at the God side of things, we will see the good, and we won't be so quick to retreat. One day he asked, "Yolanda, if you knew you couldn't lose, would you take on a football team?" I guess the hesitation in my voice was enough to express my apprehension. So he rebutted by saying, "There's a protection that God gives His children that enables us to win every time. Even our losses are gains because God makes everything work!"

Psalm 73:23–24 reads, "I am always with you; you hold me by my right hand. You guide me with your counsel, and afterward you will take me into glory" (NIV). These words are the promise that God is watching over us. He is protecting us. He has the complete vision of our lives and will faithfully take us from beginning to end!

Point of Prayer

God, thank You for Your unceasing protection. I know You are always with me, not only watching but waiting to keep me safe from harm. In You I can walk in confidence and assurance that

I can handle anything I encounter, and everything is as it is supposed to be.

10 Pensive Points

The vision of God as our constant protector is the ultimate comfort. Knowing that the Lord is always with us no matter what we face is more evidence of the Holy Spirit's amazing power. Even when we are not aware of Him, God is working to keep us safe. God is an awesome God.

1. Think back to a near-disaster from which God delivered you.
2. Besides prayer, how do you show God your trust?
3. Make a list as long as you can of the small ways you trust God.
4. What is preventing you from relying on God in large ways?
5. Look at your list of small things and circle items that might help you increase your reliance on God.
6. On a scratch pad, draw the way you see God as a protector.
7. Think of the songs you like and choose one that reminds you that God is ever watchful and responsive. Memorize its words and melody.
8. Think of situations in which you're most inclined to rely on your own instincts.
9. Write down those situations, each prefaced by "I used to...," and end each statement with what you will do to step out into the uncharted territory of faith. (For example: "I used to stay up until all hours of the night waiting for my teenage son to come home, until I put on the song 'God Is' and got in bed and fell asleep trusting Jesus to protect my boy.")

10. Whom do you know who confidently finds safety in His protection? Ask that person to be your "Point of Power" partner and encourage you when you need it.

Power Passage

I will remain in the world no longer, but they are still in the world, and I am coming to you. Holy Father, protect them by the power of your name—the name you gave me—so that they may be one as we are one. While I was with them, I protected them and kept them safe by that name you gave me. None has been lost except the one doomed to destruction so that Scripture would be fulfilled. (John 17:11–12 NIV)

God's Constant Protection Is Relentless, Faithful, Perfect

He is my constant in a wavering world.

We've heard people say, "I'll always be there." This statement appears in dialogue between friends and family, between close companions, and between partners in new relationships. And while we say it with the best of intentions, we also say it with the understanding that we are prone to bouts of inconsistency, selfishness, and temperament. Because of schedules, plans, and obligations, we may not always be able to be there. But when God promises us that He'll always be there, the Lord's word is true. The Holy Spirit's protection for our lives is relentless, faithful, and perfect.

It was hard when my second marriage ended. I thought I'd be married to my husband forever. He and I had been friends for a long time. I am a very private person and rarely discuss the specifics and particulars of my private life because I believe some things only God should know. I share this experience, however, to encourage anyone with a broken heart. Understand that God will protect you and help you heal if you let Him.

When you experience a divorce or the end of a trusted relationship it's normal to start second-guessing everything. You second-guess your love, your compassion, and yourself. One of my good friends, Super Bowl champion Daryl Haley, helped me when he said, "Remember, it wasn't you!" God kept trying to remind me that the Lord shielded me from devastation. It took encouragement from people I love and trust to reassure me of what God had already put in my heart.

Fast-forward to the present: I am so grateful. I would have missed some amazing moments had I not gone through that rough time. Now I have the most amazing little eight-year-old girl. I have great family and friends. I work with the best morning crew in the world on a nationally syndicated radio show! So take it from me, God helps you find protection in His love. Something wonderful is on the other side of your pain. Believe and trust God for the best, and you will have it in your life!

When I recall stories of protection in the Bible, few resonate with me more than the story of Daniel in the lions' den. It's a stunning example of the protection we enjoy as a result of our faith in God.

Daniel was a man who had enjoyed God's favor. He served in the king's courts and powerfully interpreted dreams. Daniel's fellow administrators in the kingdom were envious of his success and authority. When King Darius came to rule, he was very impressed with Daniel, who at that point served as one of three administrators over the kingdom. He set himself apart so much that the king considered giving Daniel control over the entire kingdom.

That made the others even more jealous, and they attempted to remove Daniel from the good graces of the king. But try as they might to find corruption in his past, they came up empty. Daniel was a righteous man who pursued truth, goodness, and the law of the Lord. The only way they could undo him was to threaten his relationship with God.

The administrators connived and asked King Darius for an edict that would prohibit anyone from praying to or worshiping anyone but Darius himself for thirty days. Those who disobeyed would be thrown into the lions' den. It would be a demonstration, they said, of Darius's power and show the people who was truly in charge. Under the pressure of his administrators and the fluffing of his ego, Darius consented and issued the edict.

Once this was done, the administrators knew it would be easy to catch Daniel. Just as he was a faithful man in his morality, he was faithful in his worship of God. Three times a day he would open his windows toward Jerusalem and pray to God in thanks. Despite Darius's edict, they knew Daniel would continue. He was fervent in his belief and wouldn't allow the new law to stop him from worshiping the One he believed in.

Soon the men found Daniel praying and brought him before the king. They told the king they had one who had disobeyed his laws. When King Darius found out it was Daniel, he was very upset. Though Darius wished to save Daniel, his administrators held him to his law and Darius consented. Before Daniel was thrown in with the lions, King Darius said, "May your God, whom you serve continually, rescue you!" (Daniel 6:16 NIV).

The entire night, the king tossed and turned in anguish. He ate no food and enjoyed no entertainment but thought in despair of his friend Daniel in the den. When morning came, he rushed down to the lions' den and yelled for Daniel, asking if indeed the Lord he worshiped had saved him. Daniel responded: "My God sent his angel, and he shut the mouths of the lions. They have not hurt me, because I was found innocent in his sight" (6:22 NIV).

King Darius was joyful at Daniel's salvation. He immediately brought him out of the den. Not a scar or wound from one of the animals was on his body. After witnessing such deliverance, King Darius threw Daniel's accusers into the pit and the lions quickly ate them. Afterward, he issued a new edict, one celebrating Daniel's God and telling all in the kingdom to worship the Lord.

Power Passage

Be strong in the Lord and in his mighty power. Put on the full armor of God so that you can take your stand against the devil's schemes. For our struggle is not against flesh and blood, but against the rulers, against the authorities, against the powers of this dark world and against the spiritual forces of evil in the heavenly realms. (Ephesians 6:10–12 NIV)

Point of Practice

Daniel's story is one of how constant faithfulness produces relentless protection. Daniel saw numerous kings. He saw empires change and kingdoms rebuilt. And while people came and went and laws were formed and broken, he remained faithful to God and God remained faithful to him. When King Darius arrived and made the decree not to worship any other gods, Daniel knew it was one law he would have to break. Time and again, people had failed and faltered, but the Lord never did. Daniel's fear of and reverence for God were greater than his fear or awe of any ruler. In the end, he knew it was better to face the lions than to face denying God.

God promises to be our constant in the same way. First Peter 5:8–9 warns, "Be self-controlled and alert. Your enemy the devil prowls around like a roaring lion looking for someone to devour. Resist him, standing firm in the faith" (NIV).

If we haven't already, we all will meet people like the administrators in Daniel's story—those who seek to do us harm and belittle our faith. But we cannot allow the words of the devil and the threat of fear to drive us to a place where we trust more in the hand of man than in the hand of God. Romans 8:31 states, "If God is for us, who can be against us?" (NIV). Rest assured in those words. We are divinely protected and divinely loved. Just as Daniel came out unscathed from a pit teeming with death and hurt, we too will be delivered from the worldly danger that threatens to consume us. Remain faithful to the Lord, and He will remain faithful to you.

Point of Prayer

God, You are awesome! I am grateful for Your powerful presence in my life. No matter what I come up against, no matter what challenge I face, I know You are beside me, strengthening me, guiding me, comforting me with Your love and faithful support and protection.

10 Pensive Points

Not everyone we encounter is going to be a believer. In fact, you may face times when your faith is not only tested but belittled. When we remain faithful in our praise and supplication of the Holy Spirit, the Lord responds with never-ending protection. As we are faithful, God is faithful to us.

1. Think of a time in your life when you were up against people like the administrators in Darius's court. What were their dominant characteristics?

2. What are some ways you can deal with people like this and remain faithful to the Lord?

3. Daniel found his constant in God. What are the constants in your life?

4. How constant is your faith?

5. Write down some ways you could show your faith in God on a regular basis.

6. What are some ways you see God's faithfulness to you in your life?

7. How often do you show gratitude for all the Lord has done for you?

8. For the next week write down five things you have to be grateful to God for each night before you go to sleep.

9. At the end of seven days, read over your entire week's list. Take in all you have in your life. Give God the praise!

10. Do you notice any circumstances or areas in which God is especially faithful to you?

Power Passage

As the heavens are higher than the earth,
   so are my ways higher than your ways
   and my thoughts than your thoughts.
(Isaiah 55:9 NIV)

I Am Grounded in the Familiar—God

I know that the Lord is always beside me.

Have you ever been stranded in a strange place? Perhaps your car broke down on the side of the road. You weren't from the area, you had no maps or GPS, your cell phone service was out, and it was getting dark. Thankfully, in your passenger-side seat you had a friend with you. What a comfort it was to know you weren't stranded in a strange place alone. Just imagine if you had been by yourself!

Like a friend in the car, God is our point of familiar. He is our steady, guiding compass when everything else feels untamed and lost. Believing in that is what makes us Christians. We trust that God exists. We know that the Lord is active and always near us from one day to the next. In my song "Through the Storm," that trust is put into words. I sing about having no fear, even when I am in the midst of the crashing waves like Jesus and the disciples on the sea. All I have to do is speak the name *Jesus*, and nothing can hurt me. When you're nervous, scared, and feeling abandoned, take heart! While you may be encountering the unknown, God is there with you and He knows no wilderness.

Scott O'Grady can speak to God's consistent presence.

When the missile hit Scott O'Grady's F-16, the impact was immediate and the plane was split in two. He was lucky to eject, but his landing wasn't as fortunate. He suffered minor burns during ejection and skyrocketed out of his plane four miles above enemy territory. On the long ride down via parachute, he saw a truck of Serbian soldiers poised in Bosnia's countryside waiting for the young American fighter pilot to land. For all intents and purposes, he was as good as gone.

When O'Grady hit the ground, he covered his skin in dirt. Everything shiny, everything white, everything bright had to go. He covered what he could and lay still on the ground as he heard the Serbian soldiers shooting at random. They hovered a mere body's length away, but they didn't find him. O'Grady was confident in his salvation. It was "God," he said. "Period."

The first day was a matter of fighting fear, thirst, and the ever-watchful search parties that dotted the landscape. He lay on the ground for five hours before moving. He had a small amount of water in his survival gear, but he slaked his thirst with dirty rainfall he sopped up in a sponge. At night, he wrapped himself in a large, waterproof sheet he had stowed in his pocket. He fended off ants. He slept near a farm where the mooing cows provided companionship, easing his tight nerves. Two bulls hung around so much he dubbed them Leroy and Alfred.

One day turned into six. He lay in the thick of the Bosnian brush, not entirely sure whether he would make it out alive, but praying for unlikely salvation. He had turned off his radio at the beginning, worried that the Serbian soldiers would hear its signal and catch wind of where he was. So as NATO combed the area for any evidence of his survival or demise, O'Grady remained largely off-line. The only leads the NATO search party had were from intercepts on the Serbian side. The verdict was in: they had O'Grady's parachute, but not the man.

When the risk wasn't as great, O'Grady finally turned on his radio. But the signal couldn't be heard very far away. U.S. forces and NATO heard fuzzy signals that could be O'Grady, but it was hard to tell. Finally, one night, the signal went through. A fellow American fighter pilot was flying above him, but his plane had less than five minutes' worth of fuel left before he would have to turn around. Just before he headed back to base, the confirmation came through. O'Grady heard three beeps on the radio and knew they were coming. "I'm alive! I'm alive!" he said. After dialoguing briefly with O'Grady, the fighter pilot returned, tears in his eyes, and a rescue mission was set for dawn.

Forty warplanes hit the sky. At six, O'Grady shot off his flare. The risk of failure was great. The Serbs knew the Americans were headed for the pilot, and if the Marines didn't get there in time and safely, O'Grady would be gone. But God was on his side. A chopper landed and O'Grady shot out of the brush and headed for safety. He was wet and weak, waving his gun in the air, but he made it.

Power Passage

The LORD Almighty is with us;
    the God of Jacob is our fortress.
    (Psalm 46:11 NIV)

Point of Practice

For six days and six nights, Scott O'Grady experienced the ultimate threat. Not only was he in an unfamiliar place alone, he was in enemy territory. He was surrounded by people who were eager to see his life come to an end. He had no food, little water, and no certain day of salvation. The situation was so fragile; he had to be intentional about his every move. Nothing rash. Nothing loud. Nothing that would call attention to him.

Despite the foreign landscape and all the unknowns, O'Grady was rescued. He was lifted from the wilderness to a place of safety and security.

When Scott O'Grady got off the plane and walked onto safe soil after a remarkable rescue, he knew immediately where the praise was due. "Right off the bat, the first thing I want to do is to thank God," he said. "If it wasn't for God's love for me and my love for God, I wouldn't have gotten through it. He's the one that delivered me here, and I know that in my heart."[1]

As with O'Grady, life's circumstances can leave us feeling abandoned. We can be in a place where we see no allies and no way out. But while we might feel as though we're floundering, God knows no wilderness. He protects us in places steeped in harm and will usher us into the grace of His salvation. Pray to Him when you feel most alone, look for survival in the seeds of potential around you, and always wait diligently to hear the Lord's answer that will keep you grounded in the familiar.

Point of Prayer

God, when I am in the wilderness of life I turn to You. Lord, take from my heart any doubt or fear. Remind me that Your faithfulness, Your love, and Your plan are always the answers I need. I don't ever need to worry or stress but only to bring my concerns and challenges to You and ask for Your guidance.

10 Pensive Points

God never leaves us. No matter what the situation, the Lord's love and protection always surround us. Trust in that and there is no need to be anxious for anything.

1. What are your thoughts about Scott O'Grady's situation?

2. Think about a time when you thought everything was lost.

3. How did you react? Did you wait patiently? Or did you plow your way ahead?

4. As you think about that time, in what ways did God protect you?

5. What roles do patience and faith play in your life?

6. Scott O'Grady was grounded in the familiar. While he was in enemy territory, he knew he was in the hand of God. How are you grounded in the familiar? How is that a source of strength for you?

7. Think of other examples of situations where you have witnessed God's protection in your life or in the life of someone you know.

8. List some of the wilderness areas currently in your life.

9. Think of three ways you could ask God for help in those areas.

10. As you see God at work in your life, write it down in your journal.

Power Passage

The LORD is my light and my salvation—
    whom shall I fear?
The LORD is the stronghold of my life—
    of whom shall I be afraid?

When evil men advance against me
    to devour my flesh,
when my enemies and my foes attack me,
    they will stumble and fall.
Though an army besiege me,
    my heart will not fear;
though war break out against me,
    even then I will be confident.
    (Psalm 27:1–3 NIV)

Chapter Ten

THE POWER OF VICTORY

"This accomplishment has been a struggle, but at the National Congress of Black Women, we have learned that it is from our struggles that we gain our victories. We never gave up no matter what stood in our way."

—Dr. E. Faye Williams[1]

My Diligence and God's Commitment Are an Unstoppable Combination

I live my best life in collaboration with God.

Have you ever thought about how God created things? Everything came to be as a result of what God said. He said, "Let there be light," and there was light. God intends for all of us to live lives of victory. We can do this by declaring out loud that no matter what we face, we are overcomers. We live best by walking in God's strength and authority, in cooperation with Him.

That's the message behind my song "Victory." It was featured on the sound track of the movie *The Gospel*. I sing about knowing that no matter what challenge I am facing, I am victorious. Jesus died on the cross for me and then rose on the third day, so there is nothing I can't do. Whenever I sing that song it reminds me that no matter what is happening in our lives, in God we always win.

But instead of believing in victory, sometimes we are guilty of couch potato belief. We bellow about our problems to God like patients on therapy couches and wait for Him to jot down a prescription. I know I've looked for the quick fix before, the easy way out. Wholeness, health, and success don't result from simply being honest with God and others. We must listen to the truth we hear and then go further and act it out. I've learned that complacency doesn't produce victorious living. My best has come through the collaborative strength of my diligence combined with God's commitment. What are *you* doing to further your role in the kingdom?

In 2001, *Time* magazine asked the question many others had been wondering: Is this man the next Billy Graham? Standing and looking at T. D. Jakes on the stage, it's hard to contend otherwise. He's packed out the 79,000-seat Georgia Dome. He's preached to George W. Bush and Al Gore. His church in south Dallas, the Potter's House, has more than 30,000 members and continues to grow. He's received 13 honorary degrees and doctorates. He's written more than 30 books and graced the *New York Times* best-seller list. He's hosted numerous conferences, has a worldwide television ministry, and is an award-winning gospel singer. It's no wonder the man draws comparison to Dr. Martin Luther King and Billy Graham.

Born Thomas Dexter Jakes on June 9, 1957, in Charleston, a coal-mining town in West Virginia, T.D. comes from humble roots. He grew up in a strict household with parents who prized hard work. His mother, Odith, was a home economics teacher; and his father, Ernest, a janitor. Jakes says he was influenced by being around blue-collar people who hustled and worked hard, especially his father.

Jakes's father didn't just tell him to work hard; he showed him proof that tireless effort and stamina pay off. He became an entrepreneur long before many African Americans were doing so and opened his own janitorial company. Starting out with little more than a mop and a bucket, he grew the company to fifty-two employees, eventually landing the state capitol as one of his clients. That hardworking, entrepreneurial spirit rubbed off on T.D., who as a child worked to earn money by delivering newspapers, selling Avon products, and selling vegetables from his mother's garden.

Church was also an important part of Jakes's life. He claims to have been a normal child who got into trouble like all kids. However, even at a young age, he felt deeply drawn to religious stories. He often carried a Bible to school with him, hence earning the nickname "Bible Boy." Because he spoke with a lisp, someone told him he would never preach, but that didn't stop him from practice-preaching to an imaginary congregation.

Jakes's childhood took a harsh turn when he was just ten years old. His father was diagnosed with chronic kidney failure. While other kids were out playing, T.D. was often inside tending to his father and mopping up the blood from the machine that was his father's lifeline. T.D.'s father died when he was sixteen. "Healing became imperative to me," he said, "to respond to a childhood I didn't have and a life I didn't get to live, growing up in hospitals and emergency rooms and [with] a kidney machine in my basement."

T.D. endured the pain of losing his father so young and soon after heeded the call to ministry. He began preaching part-time while he worked at other jobs to make ends meet. Eventually he caught the attention of a young lady named Serita, who, impressed by his ministry, started sending him anonymous cards of encouragement. Finally the two met and eventually married.

In 1980, Jakes eventually established and chartered Temple of Faith, a small storefront church in a former garage in West Virginia, with ten members. He even dug ditches to supplement his income while building his ministry. While in West Virginia he also began his first radio ministry, held his first conference, and in 1992 first preached the sermon "Woman, Thou Art Loosed" to a Sunday school class of about fifteen women. The book of the same name (it also became a successful movie) encouraged women to rise above sexual abuse, degradation, violence, and insecurities. Jakes so believed in the book's message that he cleaned out his personal bank account to publish it. It struck a chord with readers and eventually sold more than three million copies.

In May 1996, after thirty-eight years spent living in West Virginia, Jakes was hungry for change. He moved his family and a group of fifty longtime church staff members and their families to Dallas. Jakes felt he was called to be there. He had the feeling the people of Dallas were hungry for what he had to say. "Cast your cares to the wind and say this is my moment and I'm not going to miss it" was his philosophy.

In Dallas Jakes founded the Potter's House, a nondenominational church based on Pentecostal beliefs. The church was an immediate success. Some fifteen hundred people joined the very first Sunday, more than he had ever preached to in his entire fifteen years of ministry in West Virginia.

In addition to the church ministry, Jakes has worked hard to get his message to people outside of and often unenthused by the traditional church. He has produced stage plays, started a television ministry seen around the world, and authored many bestselling books based on his popular sermons. Known for his "tell it like it is" style, Jakes takes the issues of the day head-on and is undeterred by the criticism he sometimes receives because of it.

Subjects like AIDS, sexual abuse, and infidelity are often part of his sermons. He believes it is important to be honest and straightforward about what is happening in the world. Jakes not only helps struggling people turn their lives around, but he also helps people save money to buy houses and send their children to college. Potter's House has established more than one hundred programs to help the community, including programs for the homeless and imprisoned, support groups for the disenfranchised, voter registration drives, and drug rehabilitation programs.

Jakes believes he is doing God's will in his work. In spite of his difficult circumstances, through his tenacity, hard work, and unwavering faith in God, T. D. Jakes keeps walking forward, discovering new ways to use his talents and gifts, and reaching out to help others and inspire them to rise above their circumstances. T. D. Jakes knows the importance of maintaining a strong connection with God in everything he does.

"I encourage people, don't die until you find that thing that you were created to do," said Jakes in an interview, "because the moment you have fulfillment and accomplishment and success comes with it, to find that thing that fills you full of gratification and makes you smile when you do it, that's rich. An accountant can never keep record on it and you don't have to pay taxes on it."[1]

Power Passage

Even youths grow tired and weary,
    and young men stumble and fall;
but those who hope in the Lord
    will renew their strength.
They will soar on wings like eagles;
    they will run and not grow weary,
    they will walk and not be faint.
(Isaiah 40:30–31 NIV)

Point of Practice

I have known Bishop T. D. Jakes for twenty years. When we met, he had not yet been named "America's Prophet" or graced the covers of hundreds of magazines. He had not yet become the pastor of a thirty-thousand-member church. But there was something in this shy minister that screamed, *Success!* It didn't surprise me when great things started happening for him. No matter what T.D. has had to face, he has approached it straight on and found a way, with God as his guide, to overcome. Success never comes without challenges and victory never comes without battles. Everyone has to press forward in order to reach his or her goal.

Jessie Duplantis is also one of my favorite preachers. He says the only time you see success before work is in the dictionary.

Everyone Jesus called to walk beside Him was working. Luke was a practicing physician. John and James were fishermen. God calls us to do the same things with our gifts as T. D. Jakes has done with his.

Just as in the parable of the talents in Matthew 25:14–30, no matter if we have five talents or only one, God expects us to use the gifts He gives us responsibly and with enthusiasm. Failure need never be a worry because God-given gifts are not ours, they are God's. We are to take good care of them, thank God for them, and use them to the best of our ability. It is our job to dig, discover, persevere, and work, just as T. D. Jakes does, to discover our gifts and talents, then put them into action as a reflection of God in the world.

Get busy doing what you love. Victory is in completing your assignments. As you complete one, God gives you more because He can trust you. Your faithfulness is tied to your victories. There's power in victory. Every success says, *If God did it before, He'll do it again!*

Point of Prayer

God, thank You for the gifts and talents You have given me. Some are large and some are small, but each one makes me uniquely me, and for that I am grateful. Every day, I am amazed to learn more about who I am, what I am good at. It seems the more I find inside me, the more I am given. I am working hard each day to stay the course, to pursue my goals and use my talents as You would have me use them. I ask You, God, to make me a good example of Your love to everyone I meet.

10 Pensive Points

No matter who you are, no matter what your circumstances, you have at least one God-given gift, one talent that is uniquely yours. Using our gifts in the world is another way of worshiping God. God expects us to share His gifts with the world. It is the way we can say "Thank You" for all we have been given.

1. T. D. Jakes's story is a striking illustration of God's diligence and commitment to His people. Think about the ways T.D. stayed diligent and committed to God in his life.

2. List three ways God has shown commitment to you.

3. What are your God-given talents?

4. Write down the things in your life that you are most committed to.

5. Compare your list of commitments and talents. Journal about how those items match up.

6. Also in your journal, formulate a prayer to ask God to help you further match your talents and dreams, and say the prayer every day for a month. After saying the prayer for a few days, do you notice any changes in the things you seem committed to?

7. Do you notice any God-given talents that you aren't using? What are they? Write in your journal about what is keeping you from pursuing them.

8. Choose one talent that you aren't using and make a plan this week to take one step toward exploring it.

9. Commit yourself to a long-term goal of ninety days to a year to take one of your talents and do something amazing with it! Share your goal with a trusted friend who will hold you accountable. Write in your journal about how you will reach your goal.

10. Once you reach your goal, write in your journal about how you feel. Use that feeling to propel yourself to use this and other talents in your life.

Power Passage

Teach me your way, O Lord;
  lead me in a straight path
  because of my oppressors.
Do not turn me over to the desire of my foes,
  for false witnesses rise up against me,
  breathing out violence.
I am still confident of this:
  I will see the goodness of the Lord
  in the land of the living.
Wait for the Lord;
  be strong and take heart
  and wait for the Lord. (Psalm 27:11–14 NIV)

My God-Given Strengths Provide the Building Blocks for My Success

God acts as my eternal support beam.

Think about the times you've had to approach difficult tasks. When you're alone, the mountain you have to climb can seem too high. Doubts about your own ability filter in and you don't know if you'll be able to make it to the next plateau, much less the summit. But God has a fervent belief in our strengths and provides us with the handholds and ledges to meet our greatest climbing challenges head-on. He brought me out of the most difficult trials in my life to the most abundant place of hope, and the Lord can do the same for you.

Lakewood Church started small. On Mother's Day in 1959 in a converted feed store, John Osteen stood in front of a small group from the Houston, Texas, area and gave the first of many sermons to the Lakewood congregation. In the coming decades Lakewood would become one of the largest churches in America with a successful television ministry and a vast community outreach.

John encouraged his son Joel to preach, but Joel preferred to stay behind the scenes. Joel worked in the television and marketing efforts of Lakewood's community, helping expand his father's reach. He finally accepted his father's invitation and preached his first sermon on January 17, 1999. His father died unexpectedly of a heart attack just a week later. Joel stepped up to be the voice of the community.

"The first year I was nervous, and I talked real fast," he says. But Osteen relied on who he was, telling stories about his family and making people laugh. After some practice he grew into the role, using his affable, gentle persona and focusing on a positive message. Joel had found his calling.

Over the next ten years, Lakewood expanded in ways John Osteen could only have imagined. The congregation grew from six thousand to forty-two thousand people, so many that Lakewood had to move into a former pro basketball arena. Annual donations were $75 million. Joel penned the best seller *Your Best Life Now*, which sold more than five million copies, and the church's sermons were broadcast all over the world.

Lakewood is now a far cry from its modest beginnings in a feed store. It's become a church built by a father and expanded by a son. It represents a new American evangelism.[1]

Power Passage

The LORD is my rock, my fortress and my deliverer;
　　my God is my rock, in whom I take refuge.
He is my shield and the horn of my salvation,
　　my stronghold. (Psalm 18:2 NIV)

Point of Practice

God calls on the most unlikely candidates to do the Lord's work. Joel had been totally satisfied serving God from behind the scenes. Stepping up to preach was probably the last thing on his mind, and the grief from his father's recent death was still very fresh. Yet he faithfully answered the Lord's call anyway.

God knows what the Lord has placed within us. The Holy Spirit expects us to be victorious with what God has given us. I am blessed by Joel every time I watch his broadcast. He is endearing in his delivery. It's as if you're listening to your favorite cousin expound on his personal experiences. As the years have passed, his strength and confidence have developed. I am so proud that he has stood by his preaching style and refused to adjust it to satisfy his critics.

I believe people are looking for true Christians who will tell it the way they've experienced it. Joel is a great example of a victorious Christian who does exactly that.

The power of victory in God is that the Lord provides us opportunities for success just as God did for Joel. The Holy Spirit doesn't care if victory seems "unlikely" or if you don't seem "fit" for the job. God sees you as a perfect creation, molded in His image, with all the strength you need coming from God's faith in you.

Point of Prayer

God, as I go through life, help me see myself as You see me. Help me uncover the gifts You have placed within me and use them according to Your will. I may not always understand why You are leading me in a certain direction, but I trust that You see abilities in me that I have yet to recognize in myself, and I step forward in faith.

10 Pensive Points

We don't always recognize our talents and abilities, but God knows we have them because He placed them in us. When the opportunity to do something new or different knocks on your door, answer it. God sent it to you to expand your life and your vision of yourself, to remind you to put your trust in the Lord.

1. Think about the ways God worked in Joel's life to help him find and answer his calling.

2. Would you be willing to faithfully answer God's call even in the midst of grief the way Joel did? Or would you make excuses and say, "Not now, God. This is not a good time"?

3. What steps did Joel take to walk toward victory?

4. What unlikely acts of victory have you seen in the lives of your family members and friends?

5. Do you have gifts God has placed in your life that are lying dormant and unused?

6. Consider the chances you've had in life to discover gifts you weren't aware of. How did you respond?

7. Take some time to get quiet and think about your current situation. How has God already shown you victory in your life?

8. If you could pursue anything right now, what would it be? What's stopping you from pursuing it right now?

9. How does your faith in God play into your idea of ultimate victory?

10. Think of something you could do today that would move you closer to your definition of victory in your life.

Power Passage

I have learned to be content whatever the circumstances. I know what it is to be in need, and I know what it is to have plenty. I have learned the secret of being content in any and every situation, whether well fed or hungry, whether living in plenty or in want. I can do everything through him who gives me strength. (Philippians 4:11–13 NIV)

My Greatest Victories Can Come in the Most Unexpected Ways

In God, I welcome the extraordinary.

God uses the unexpected in our lives so we will learn to totally depend on Him. Every day God continues to surprise me. Answers and solutions come in a variety of ways—I started out wanting to be a broadcaster and ended up in a classroom. I was teaching school and then found myself in concert halls singing in front of thousands of people. There are so many other examples I could give to show the wonderful and awesome victories God has gifted to me. The point is, being open to God is being open and available to the unexpected. Be willing to see how the Lord can use the unlikely in your life to bring you the greatest victories of all.

The Israelites' first conquest in taking Canaan was the city of Jericho. As covered earlier in this book (see Point of Power #8), Joshua sent two spies into the city who were able to gain valuable information and protection from a woman named Rahab. When the spies returned to Joshua, the spies gave him the good news that the Lord was with them and the people inside Jericho were extremely fearful of the approaching Israelites.

With news of the Lord's support, Joshua and the tribes prepared for invasion. About forty thousand Israelites, armed and ready for battle, crossed the Jordan and set foot on the other side. They camped nearby and prepared for battle.

While Joshua stood looking at the city he was to conquer, he was approached by a messenger of the Lord and told how he would go on to defeat Jericho:

> March around the city once with all the armed men. Do this for six days. Have seven priests carry trumpets of rams' horns in front of the ark. On the seventh day, march around the city seven times, with the priests blowing the trumpets. When you hear them sound a long blast on the trumpets, have all the people give a loud shout; then the wall of the city will collapse and the people will go up, every man straight in. (Joshua 6:3–5 NIV)

Joshua did as he was told. He spread the Lord's message to the people and they marched around Jericho. On the seventh day, they blew their trumpets and the walls fortifying the great city fell, and the people were delivered into the hands of the Israelites. Joshua and his men burned the city to the ground and spared no one except Rahab and her household, because she had shown mercy and kindness to the Israelites. Jericho became a city of the Lord.

Power Passage

"To whom will you compare me?
Or who is my equal?" says the Holy One.

Lift your eyes and look to the heavens:
>   Who created all these?
He who brings out the starry host one by one,
>   and calls them each by name.
Because of his great power and mighty strength,
>   not one of them is missing. (Isaiah 40:25–26 NIV)

Point of Practice

As a musician, I think the Jericho story is one of my favorite accounts in the Bible. Can you imagine singers having to be quiet for six days? It absolutely goes against our constitution. But when God asks you to do something out of the ordinary, it's because the ultimate victory is extraordinary. No matter how unusual the request, God's way is always the way of certain victory. I love that we always win in God's plan.

The lesson of Jericho is the lesson of God's prevailing wisdom. His ways, I'm thankful to say, do not mirror ours. He sees solutions we can never fathom and ways to victory we could never compose. Isaiah 55:8–9 reads, " 'My thoughts are not your thoughts, neither are your ways my ways,' declares the LORD. 'As the heavens are higher than the earth, so are my ways higher than your ways and my thoughts than your thoughts' " (NIV).

Joshua was a man of belief. He had experienced the Lord's guidance and trusted that the Lord's ways were not only different, but better. As a result of his faith, the walls of Jericho fell and the great city was delivered into Joshua's hands. The next time you find yourself head-to-head in a difficult battle, stop relying solely on your own plans, be faithful in prayer and in belief, and the walls standing before you too shall fall flat.

Point of Prayer

God, Your will be done. I prayerfully discuss my life's joys and challenges with You, God. I take all actions necessary to reach my goals. And then I faithfully listen for Your voice, knowing and trusting You will guide me in the right direction.

10 Pensive Points

God answers prayer. When we faithfully place our joys and cares into the Lord's hands, God always shows us the way. Sometimes the answers don't arrive looking as we thought they would, but they always come, and they are the right answers, the God-given answers uniquely right for us.

1. Reflect on Joshua's strong faith in God's words.

2. What made God decide the Israelites were ready to enter the promised land?

3. What role does God's voice play in your life right now?

4. Do you think your mind is clear enough to hear God's voice when He speaks to you?

5. If you answered yes, write down things God is telling you about your life today. Then write down the things you are doing to honor the Lord's voice.

6. If you answered no, what might you do to clear space to let God's voice in? Are there things you need to stop doing? Things you need to start doing?

7. Write down three things you can do or eliminate this week to make room for unexpected victory in your life.

8. Jot down some unexpected victories you have already witnessed in your life or in the lives of people you know.

9. Are you ready for the promised land in your own life? If not, why not?

10. What can you do today to get closer to your promised land?

Power Passage

If anyone is in Christ, he is a new creation; the old has gone, the new has come! (2 Corinthians 5:17 NIV)

Notes

CHAPTER ONE

1. Pamela Foster, "Yolanda Adams Live," *Tennessee Tribune*, October 23, 1996.

Point of Power #2

1. William Henry Monk (music, 1861) and Henry Francis Lyte (words, 1847), "Abide with Me," 1847, www.hymnsite.com/lyrics/umh700.sht.

Point of Power #4

1. Sources of information about Coach Don Meyer in this section include Bob McClellan, "Legendary Coach Bob Meyer Has Cancer," September 12, 2008, http://collegebasketball.rivals.com/content.asp?CID=849757; Megan Myers, "Injured Coach Has Cancer," *Argus Leader*, September 13, 2008; Myron P. Medcalf, "Gopher's Men's Basketball," *Star Tribune* (Minneapolis), November 6, 2008; Andy Rennecke, "This Coach Has Been Through Wringer," *St. Cloud Times* (Minnesota), November 24, 2008.

CHAPTER TWO

1. Michelle Bearden, "Heart Full of Soul," *Tampa Tribune*, May 10, 2002.

Point of Power #7

1. Sources of information about Kirsten Haglund included in this section include Korie Wilkins, "Overcoming Anorexia," *Times of Trenton*

(New Jersey), April 14, 2009; Jack Komperda, "Miss America Helps Teens Fight Eating Disorders," *Daily Herald* (Arlington Heights, Illinois), May 4, 2008; Ryan Nakashima, "Miss America Once Fought Anorexia," *Charleston Daily Mail*, 2008; "The International Neuromodulation Society Announces Promising Results for Treating Anorexia Nervosa with Deep Brain Stimulation," Business Wire, 2007; Korie Wilkins, "Former Miss America Goes on the Road to Try to Help Others with Eating Disorders," *Times of Trenton* (New Jersey), April 14, 2009.

CHAPTER THREE

1. Melody K. Hoffman, "Yolanda Adams: Translating God's Message into Music," *Jet*, December 12, 2005.

Point of Power #9

1. Sources of information about Nelson Mandela in this section include "A Monument to Mandela: The Robben Island years Freedom's champion," Independent on Sunday, Independent News & Media, 2007, http://www.independent.co.uk/news/world/africa/a-monument-to-mandela-the-robben-island-years-401137.html; Anton Ferreira, "Mandela's Old Jail Opened to Public; Former Prisoners, Guards Guide Tourists Around Robben Island," *Washington Post*, January 2, 1997; Ben Johnson, "The Politics of Race Abroad," *Chicago Sun-Times*, May 10, 1994; Anthony Sampson, "The Man Who Forgave His Jailers," *Interview*, September 1, 1999.

Point of Power #11

1. Information about Ryan Aldridge and Katy Hutchison in this section from Seamus O'Regan, interview with Katy Hutchison, author of *Walking After Midnight*, *Canada AM*, CTV, September 27, 2006.
2. Sources of information about Dick Fiske and Zenji Abe in this section include Heather Wadowski, "Reliving Our Nations Darkest Hours," Suite 101, http://www.suite101.com/article.cfm/red_carpet_reviews/74603/1; Ken Belson, "Japanese Veteran's Path to Reconciliation," *New York Times*, September 22, 2002; Mary Vorsino, "Pearl Harbor Veteran Bridged the Ocean to Forge Friendship with Former Enemies," *Honolulu Star-Bulletin*, April 5, 2004.

Point of Power #15

1. Sources of information about Bill Wilson in this section include Christine Gibson, "How Bill Wilson Invented Alcoholics Anonymous," June 10, 2006,http://www.americanheritage.com/articles/web/20060610-alcohol ics-anonymous-bill-wilson-bob-smith-alcoholism-oxford-group-fra nk-buchman.shtml; *Pass It On: The Story of Bill Wilson and How the A.A. Message Reached the World* (New York: Alcoholics Anonymous World Services, 1984); Susan Cheever, "Heroes & Icons: Bill Wilson," June 14, 1999, http://www.time.com/time/time100/heroes/profile/wilson01.html; Doug Wagner, review of *My Name Is Bill: Bill Wilson: His Life and the Creation of Alcoholics Anonymous*, by Susan Cheever (New York: Simon & Schuster, 2004), in *Journal of Alcohol & Drug Education*, September 2004.

Point of Power #16

1. Sources of information about Ashley Smith and Brian Nichols in this section include Lloyd DeVries, "Atlanta Hostage Recounts Ordeal," March 14, 2005, http://www.cbsnews.com/stories/2005/03/14/national/main679837 .shtml; Opray Winfrey, interview with Ashley Smith and Rick Warren, *Oprah Winfrey Show*, CBS, September 28, 2005, transcript at http://www .saddlebackfamily.com/home/images/OprahTranscriptAshleyRW.pdf.

CHAPTER FIVE

1. Ed Gordon, interview with Yolanda Adams on her new CD *Day by Day*, *News & Notes with Ed Gordon*, NPR, August 30, 2005.

Point of Power #17

1. Judy Wells, "Sky's the Limit: Jacksonville Native Carla Harris a Go-Getter from the Get-Go," *Florida Times-Union*, May 20, 2007.

Point of Power #20

1. Sources of information about Randy Pausch in this section include Beth Murtagh, "CMU Remembers Randy Pausch," *Pittsburgh Business Times*, September 23, 2008; Guy Adams, "Randy Pausch: Professor Famous for His 'Last Lecture,'" *Independent* (London), July 30, 2008,

http://www.independent.co.uk/news/obituaries/randy-pausch-profes
sor-famous-for-his-last-lecture-880271.html;RamitPlushnick-Masti, "Randy
Pausch, 47; Computer Professor's 'Last Lecture' " Became Internet Sensation,"
Boston Globe, July 26, 2008; Randy Pausch's Web site, http://download.srv
.cs.cmu.edu/~pausch/.

CHAPTER SIX

1. Fanny J. Crosby (words) and Phoebe P. Knapp (music), "Blessed Assurance," 1873.

Point of Power #21

1. Sources of information about Billy Graham in this section include Timo
Pokki, *America's Preacher and His Message: Bill Graham's View of Conver-
sion and Sanctification* (Lanham, MD: University Press of America, 1999);
Denton Lotz, "Billy Graham: An Appreciation," *Baptist History and Heri-
tage*, June 22, 2006; Kyra Phillips, *CNN Presents*, "Encore Presentation:
Billy Graham, America's Pastor," September 10, 2006; Nancy Gibbs and
Richard N. Ostling, "God's Billy Pulpit," *TIME*, November 15, 1993; Scott
Simon, "Billy Graham and the Lives God Touched," NPR *Weekend Edi-
tion*, November 8, 2008; Barry Horstman, "Billy Graham: A Man with a
Mission," *Cincinnati Post*, June 27, 2002.

Point of Power #23

1. Katisha Capers, Letters to the Editor: "The Gospel Soul of Yolanda Adams,"
Ebony, October 2000.
2. Patricia Lyons, Letters to the Editor: "Yolanda Adams," *Ebony*, November
2000.
3. Coletha Albert, "Roar of the Crowd: Praise Be to Yolanda Adams," *Texas
Monthly*, October 2007.
4. Information about Martin Luther King in this section is from Dexter King,
"King: Montgomery to Memphis," CNN, *CNN Perspectives*, April 12, 1998.

Point of Power #25

1. Information about Aron Ralston in this section is from Patricia Sheridan, "Patricia Sheridan's Breakfast with ... Aron Ralston," *Pittsburgh Post-
Gazette*, September 24, 2007).

Point of Power #26

1. "From Living in a Restroom to Making Millions: One Man's Rags to Riches Story," *20/20*, January 17, 2003, ABC News Transcripts; Ed Gordon, "A Homeless Father's 'Pursuit of Happyness,'" *News and Notes with Ed Gordon*, NPR, June 1, 2006.
2. Mark J. Konkol, "Jesus Loves Me. He Only Likes You": Chris Gardner Talks About Keys to Success, and the Pursuit of Happiness," *Chicago Sun Times* Blog, December 15, 2006.

Point of Power #28

1. Sources of information about Michael Phelps in this section include Alex Brown, "Is This the Genetic Flaw That Makes Phelps the Greatest?" *Sydney Morning Herald* (Australia), August 16, 2008; Brenda Brissette Mata, "Phelps Folly Proves He's Just Human," *Flint Journal* (Michigan), February 10, 2009; Lynn Zinser, "Mazda Asks, and Phelps Apologizes to Chinese," *New York Times*, February 14, 2009; Megan Hess, "Champion for a Cause," *Parent & Child*, http://tinyurl.com/o4d9lp; Michael Winerip, "Phelps' Mother Recalls Helping Her Son Find Gold Medal Focus," *New York Times*, http://www.nytimes.com/2008/08/10/sports/olympics/10Rparent.html?_r=4&oref=slogi%09n.

Point of Power #29

1. Sources of information about Robin Roberts in this section include Robin Roberts, *From the Heart: Eight Rules to Live By* (New York: Hyperion, 2008); George Vecsey, "TV Anchor Refuses to Yield in Battle Against Cancer," *New York Times*, July 28, 2008; Holly G. Miller, "Robin's Rules of Order," *Saturday Evening Post*, September 22, 2008; Michael Star, "Robin Wigs Out," *New York Post*, April 22, 2008, http://www.nypost.com/seven/04222008/tv/robin_wigs_out_107626.htm; Robin Roberts, "ABC's Robin Roberts: I Have Cancer," ABC, August 3, 2007,http://abcnews.go.com/GMA/CancerPreventionAndTreatment/story?id=3430554.

Point of Power #34

1. Sources of information about Scott O'Grady in this section include "The Counter-Attack of God," *Economist* (US), July 8, 1995; and Evan Thomas, "An American Hero," *Newsweek*, June 19, 1995.

CHAPTER TEN

1. PR Newswire, "Sojourner Truth Becomes First African American Woman with a Memorial in United States Capitol," April 22, 2009. Dr. E. Faye Williams, Esq., National Chair of NCBW, speaking at the dedication of the bust of Sojourner Truth, who became the first African American woman with a memorial in the United States Capitol. Yolanda was a featured performer at the event.

Point of Power #35

1. Sources of information about T. D. Jakes in this section include Kyra Phillips, "Profiles of T. D. Jakes, Billy Graham," CNN, *People in the News*, December 25, 2004; Paul Erebuwa and Lillian Okenwa, "Nigeria: Revolutionary on the Pulpit," *Africa News*, December 1, 2000; T. D. Jakes Web site, "Biography," http://www.tdjakes.com/site/PageServer?pagename=about _biography; David Van Biema, "Spirit Raiser," *TIME*, September 17, 2001, http://www.time.com/time/magazine/article/0,9171,1000836-3,00.html.

Point of Power #36

1. Sources of information about Joel Osteen in this section include "Joel Osteen: The Man Behind the Ministry," *Nightline*, ABC News, http://abc news.go.com/Nightline/story?id=2086670; Joel Osteen Ministries, http:// www.joelosteen.com/Pages/Index.aspx; Jennifer Mathieu, "Power House," *Houston Press*, April 4, 2002, http://www.houstonpress.com/2002-04-04/ news/power-house/.